LOST AMERICA

From the Atlantic to the Mississippi

LOST AMERICA

From the Atlantic to the Mississippi

Constance M. Greiff

with a Foreword by James Biddle

WEATHERVANE BOOKS   New York

DETAIL, Pennsylvania Station, New York, New York, 1906/10-1963/6,
McKim, Mead and White.

Contents

Foreword

The measure of the land and the measure
of man is the same.
— *Chief Joseph of the Nez Percé, 1877*

With the publication of *Lost America, From the Atlantic to the Mississippi*, Americans are presented both a melancholy event and a hopeful sign. *Lost America* graphically chronicles the disappearance of a nation's architectural heritage. In viewing the book, one feels a sense of sadness through a new awareness of the quality and extent of our loss. So much is gone that was meaningful to Americans in the past; so much is gone that could have been of value to present and future generations. But this book not only honors our lost cultural heritage; it also calls attention to the increasing number of preservationists and their changing role.

We are no longer unaware of the pressures brought about by rapid change in every aspect of life—nowhere more visible than in our changing landscape. Technological advance is visible even in the demolition business. Demolition experts boast now that in eight seconds a large structure can be dynamited into a mushroom cloud, before it settles into a heap of debris—as opposed to the two or three weeks required for such a feat in the recent past by conventional methods.

Whether we wish to be known as the Space Age or the Computer Age, the rapidity of change has forced Americans, out of a sense of individual and national survival, into a period of environmental understanding. Not just natural elements form that environment, but man-made objects as well. The structures in which man lives and works are important along with the air he breathes and the water he uses. We pollute our air and water; our hearing is impaired by excessive and unpleasant noise; and our aesthetic sensibility is polluted by the rapidly deteriorating urban and rural setting through which we move every day. Conservation of our cultural assets, though not a household concept yet, is certainly a national issue along with conservation of our natural assets.

The interest shown in the preparation of this volume is further testimony to the resolve and skill with which thousands of men and women are waging battle against the bulldozer. Several hundred historical and preservation groups, including the National Trust for Historic Preservation, have taken the time to submit photographs and drawings for *Lost America*.

A few of these valuable buildings were destroyed by fire or other natural causes. In retrospect, even these might be standing today if simple procedures of building maintenance had been followed. However, the majority of the structures were willfully neglected or overtly destroyed. Among these are the landmark houses, schools, churches, the pleasurable amenities of city and village, and the entertaining architectural novelties that harmonized with the landscape and provided a cultural measure of man's best nature. All might have been put to constructive use today.

That these buildings were not reused or adapted to a new function 100, 20 or just 10 years ago is a shameful waste and a sad commentary on our way of life, a characteristic that is even more intensified today. In days gone by, preservationists turned civic buildings and stately houses into museums of an event or monuments to their ancestors. Some believed that all they had to do to serve their cause was to restore a nice old house, furnish it with reasonable authenticity, throw open the doors and wait for a rush of visitors who would pay the admission charges that would provide the funds for maintenance and future protection. This attempt proved to be insufficient and inadequate as a national preservation program. Meanwhile, significant parts of our structural environment, that in which man spends 80 percent of his time, were left uncared for and unprotected. In 1966 it was established that one-half of the 12,000 buildings recorded since 1934 by the Historic American Buildings Survey had been destroyed. You will find many of them in these pages.

Do we have to build a new interstate highway through a district of historic or architecturally-significant and structurally-sound houses? Is it really necessary to bulldoze a colonial stone farmhouse and its surrounding grove of pines in order to erect flimsy bungalows for those leaving the city? The circle is a truly vicious one, and some way must be found to escape from it before there is nothing of value left to use and enjoy in the man-made and the natural environment.

We must seek a greater appreciation and understanding of the many cultures and styles that have formed the American cultural heritage—from the Atlantic to the Pacific. In today's world, there is little place for ancestor worship, preservation for the sake of one's class or ethnic group. As Constance Grieff notes in her Introduction, buildings in America have had to earn their keep. To prove to our fellow Americans the very real cultural and environmental value of thousands of structures and styles threatened with destruction each year is the very difficult task ahead of us. When you go to City Hall or the State Capitol, you will have to prove, as architectural critic Ada Louise Huxtable has written, that you are "dealing with reality, not a pink or white elephant."

"Ecology Sells Well—If It's Convenient" states a recent headline in *The New York Times*. So does preservation—if it isn't a nuisance. Just about everyone enjoys having a familiar landmark around — an old hotel, courthouse, Victorian house, little red schoolhouse, covered bridge. More of us today are prepared to argue effectively that buildings inherited from the past can play a vital role in our day-to-day life. The old railroad station can become a dress shop; a house, a school; a movie house, a symphony hall; a church, a restaurant; a school house, an office. These are a few of the thousands of examples that have been developed; endless combinations can evolve with time and imagination.

As our knowledge of what cultural heritage is and our need for it has deepened, so have we gained new tools in the fight for preservation and learned to use more effectively those we already possessed. The National Historic Preservation Act of 1966, administered by the U. S. Department of the Interior, established a greatly expanded National Register of Historic Places. It lists more than 3,000 places — districts, structures, sites, buildings and objects of national, state and local significance — and grows daily. State Liaison Officers and review boards of qualified professionals were appointed by each governor following the 1966 act to gather the necessary documentation on landmarks, create state registers and pass on landmark nominations to the National Register. State preservation surveys and plans have been prepared. Federal matching funds are available under the 1966 act for surveys, plans and "brick and mortar" projects. Open space, preservation and survey funds are also available from the U. S. Department of Housing and Urban Development.

The National Trust has broadened its technical services to assist private citizens in the use of these government programs and administers a program of consultant grants, technical advice and publications, regional seminars and educational training conferences. Legal experts are today prepared to offer useful assistance in the expanding field of preservation law, a service that has been fostered by the National Trust. In spite of all these aids, the saving of a landmark remains very much a local matter.

Consider the case of Olana, that Moorish fantasy of a house, high above the Hudson River, designed by and built for artist Frederic E. Church in 1870. It was during the battle to save this house in 1965 and 1966 that I learned first-hand the ways and wiles of historic preservation.

Olana first and foremost was saved by private endeavor — not by one individual but by group action, lead by Olana Preservation, Inc., using many techniques. The initial endeavor was to persuade the heirs of the great house and its collections to grant sufficient time for the committee to acquire the whole. Auction tags were on everything and the pictures had already been shipped to New York City. We were told it was too late to stop, but stop it we did with persuasive words. We were given less than a year to raise $470,000 in exchange for Olana and its contents.

The next step was to organize a New York City committee to coordinate the efforts of many local committees that were being set up in the communities and counties near Olana. The New York City committee's chief responsibility was to find the big money; the local committees baked cakes, held bazaars and fashion shows — all intended to arouse the countryside. Why arouse the countryside? Therein were the votes and we needed votes. In the event that we were unable to raise private funds to save Olana, we had a bill introduced into the New York State Legislature authorizing the funds to acquire it.

The deadline was approaching. Although our publicity had been excellent, practically all the money, approximately $300,000, was raised from a few major donors and we were still very short of our goal. Our bill had bogged down in committee and would not reach the floor of the legislature in time to meet our deadline. Discretion intervenes here to fog the political debts the committee and its contacts called due. The bill did reach the floor and was passed, private and public money having joined to purchase Olana. Rather than becoming just another entry in *Lost America*, Olana became a property of the people of New York and the nation to study and enjoy for many years.

This volume, and the one to come on the states west of the

Mississippi — *Lost America, From the Mississippi to the Pacific* — will say more to you than any lecture I or any other preservationist can deliver. Olana and a thousand other successful battles prove that preservation can be achieved only if people care. Gone forever, however, are New York City's Pennsylvania Station, Louisiana's Belle Grove, Hoboken's Stevens Castle, Grand Rapids' City Hall, Buffalo's Larkin Building, Chicago's Schiller Building (Garrick Theater). We must care enough to inspire others to join the preservation ranks — intelligent and enthusiastic action can provide the means of saving and integrating the past with the present. There is no way to revive *Lost America*, but we can work harder to evaluate and save that which remains; there is no time to lose!

JAMES BIDDLE

James Biddle is President of the National Trust for Historic Preservation. The National Trust was created in 1949 by a charter from the United States Congress. It is the only national private organization charged with the responsibility to encourage public participation in the preservation of districts, structures, sites, buildings and objects significant in American history and culture.

Introduction

When the first European settlers set foot on the American continent, they began to destroy as surely as they began to build a new civilization. In the act of building, they eroded the wilderness. And in their quest for more land, they first disrupted and then destroyed the man-made traces of the aboriginal civilizations that preceded theirs. By the late seventeenth century the Indian villages of coastal Virginia and the Carolinas had, like most of their inhabitants, been eradicated.

The early arrivals at each new American frontier wasted no more thought on the abandonment or destruction of their own first shelters than they did on those of the Indians. There was no nostalgia, no desire to preserve the crude huts of Plimoth Plantation or the rude caves hacked out of the banks of the Delaware at Philadelphia. They were deserted, with no regrets, as soon as the settlers could erect more substantial housing. Some of the one and two-room houses built along the eastern seaboard and in the Mississippi Valley during the seventeenth and early eighteenth centuries were more enduring. Their survival, occasionally intact, more often integrated into or as an adjunct to a later structure, generally depended on whether they were well-built and continued to be useful as shelter.

The design of buildings is unique among the arts. Art historians and critics may elevate architecture to equal status in the trilogy of the artistic pantheon. The standard fine arts curriculum may read — as if in one breath — painting, sculpture and architecture. But unlike a picture or a statue, a building must continue to justify itself on more than artistic grounds — especially so in America. It must continue, in some way, to be functional if it is to survive. And only recently have Americans begun to accept the notion that function might include the provision of visual delight, variety in the townscape, or a sense of place and identity. The basic criterion for the choice between survival and destruction has been — as it often continues to be — economic. A building has to earn its keep.

That simple dictum has governed the attitude of most Americans towards architecture. In any contest between Mammon and Clio and whatever gods or saints watch over architects and their creations, Mammon has usually won hands down. Consider the case of Ben Franklin and his fine Philadelphia townhouse, erected in 1765 on a mid-block lot extending from Market to Chestnut

An Indian village in the Carolinas from Thomas Hariot's "A briefe and true report of the new found land of Virginia." Frankfort, 1590. Engraving by Theodore De Bry based on John White's watercolor.

Paul Revere engraving, "Boston Massacre." State Street, 1770.

"Head of State Street," a painting by James Marston, c. 1800.

State Street, c. 1850. Left, Merchants Exchange; right, Suffolk Bank.

State Street, c. 1880.

Streets. Franklin sowed the seeds of the building's destruction by having it placed at the end of a cul-de-sac entered from Market Street, reserving the valuable lots on either side of the entrance for commercial development. After his death in 1790, the house was occasionally occupied by descendants. More often it was rented, at first to M. La Cheva Frieve, the Portuguese ambassador, and then, with ever-declining status, as a school, boarding house and coffee house. The address by the second decade of the nineteenth century was, obviously, no longer a fashionable one for a residence. Nevertheless, the property was valuable since it lay near the heart of the city's financial and commercial district. Some of the busiest docks in what was still the country's major port were less than four blocks away. The country's most important financial institution, Stephen Girard's Bank, was even closer. The one obstacle to more lucrative development of the Franklin land was the house. Accordingly, in 1812, Franklin's heirs had the building demolished, continued the alley through from Market to Chestnut, and lined it with a double row of small, and presumably profitable, brick tenements. In turn, these were superseded by taller buildings in the second half of the nineteenth century.

The destruction of older buildings, in successive layers, in order to build anew on the same site, has certainly not been confined to Philadelphia. Major areas at the core of almost every American city rise today on the buried remnants of their past. They have been, to use a term currently fashionable in another context, recycled, not once, but many times. If Paul Revere, or rather his ghost, had returned to Boston in 1850, he would have had almost as much trouble recognizing parts of his city as he would today. The State Street that he carefully delineated as the background for his engraving of the Boston Massacre had itself been massacred. The decorous and dormered Georgian buildings of colonial Boston were gone. Their place had been taken by monumental Grecian temples to commerce, of which the most striking, the Merchant's Exchange and the Suffolk Bank, were the work of the greatest of Boston's Greek Revival architects, Isaiah Rogers. By the third quarter of the nineteenth century, these, in turn, were coming down, to be replaced by larger and more exuberant Victorian buildings. And, now, the process continues as those give way to the steel and glass constructions of a new classicism. Through it all the one constant reference point has been the Old State House, built in 1713 as a replacement for the Town House of 1657 that burned in 1711.

When Ben Franklin's house was razed in 1812, no voice was heard deploring the loss of the home of the father of half the cultural institutions of Philadelphia and the godfather of the Revolution. The idea of preserving the home of such a man as a public shrine simply did not occur to anyone. With equal equanimity, in the same year, Philadelphians witnessed the demolition of the original wings of Independence Hall, and the substitution of a pair of fireproof buildings designed by Robert Mills. In 1816, however, indignant protest was expressed at the loss of one part of this historic hall. It was occasioned by the stripping of the original decoration from the rooms in which the Declaration of Independence had been signed and the Constitutional Convention had sat. The project was evidently a colossal boondoggle, undertaken, according to the *Democratic Press*, to provide a job for one of the county commissioner's relatives. John Read, Jr., a member of the city's Select Council, expressed the distress and outrage of himself and a number of his fellow citizens:

"It would have particularly gratified us, to have perceived entire, every ornament & decoration, which had been placed in the building, by a correct architectural taste, particularly in that department of it, in which the declaration of independence, & the federal Constitution, were devised and completed. But we were too late to stop the manation (ruination?), which had begun and progressed, before our knowledge of it, and when we sought to recover the panelling and ornaments, to replace them, we were told that they were defaced and sold."

The sense of loss was not confined to the inhabitants of Philadelphia. In 1819 Col. John Trumbull, the painter, visited the building and noted, ". . . the alterations which have been made in the Room where Congress actually sat on the famous 4th of July are such that the picture [his "The Declaration of Independence"] cannot be hung in it . . . . The spirit of innovation [had] laid unhallowed hands upon it, and violated its venerable walls by modern improvement, as it is called."

Independence Hall was, of course, a singular building. Dismay at the violence done it did not extend to any desire to protect other American architectural monuments. It was not until mid-century that the preservation, or rather salvation, of old buildings began to merit serious consideration. By then, at the height of the romantic era, the nation's own past was beginning to exert a strong attraction. Already, in the 1820's, Washington Irving and James Fenimore Cooper had published highly romanticized versions of regional history and folklore. Serious attention was also being paid to the collection and preservation of the raw material of the country's history. Citizens' groups in state after state founded historical societies. Massachusetts, in 1791, and New York, in 1804, were a precocious vanguard of the movement. It was probably the visit of the Marquis de Lafayette, in 1824, with its evocative associations with the Revolution, that gave impetus to the founding of state historical societies in Pennsylvania (1824), Connecticut (1825), and Michigan (1826). The roster continued to grow through the first half of the century, joined by Virginia (1831), Georgia (1839), Maryland (1844), New Jersey (1845) and others.

Concomitant with the effort to assemble the documentary record, there arose some interest, however flickering and feeble, in the sites at which the drama of American history had been played out. Even in the early years of the nineteenth century the loss of a few key buildings was simply not acceptable. When Princeton's Nassau Hall burned in 1802, alumni and friends of the college promptly raised the money to rebuild it. Congress, returning to the hulk of the Capitol after the War of 1812, briefly debated starting afresh on the flats near the Potomac. Fortunately it was decided to rebuild on the hill that the city's designer, Pierre L'Enfant, had likened to "a pedestal waiting for a monument." Philadelphians, rallying from their shock over the destruction of the interior of the Assembly Room of Independence Hall, commissioned John Haviland to undertake the first of a series of restorations in 1824.

So there were scattered votes against the abandonment of important buildings that had been damaged. But there were no advocates for buildings that were simply either old or beautiful.

The first organized attempt at saving a building came, appropriately enough, from Massachusetts, which, as one of the oldest and most thickly settled areas on the eastern seaboard, was following one of the basic and seemingly inexorable laws governing the fate of architecture. Those areas that have the most to lose, lose the most. Their losses are perhaps less tragic than those of an area like,

Old Indian House, Deerfield, Massachusetts, 1698–1848.

Hancock House, Boston, 1737/46–1863.

Jonathan Hasbrouck House (Washington's Headquarters), Newburgh, New York, 1727/70/80.

Pumping Station, Philadelphia Waterworks, Centre Square, 1799–1827, Benjamin Henry Latrobe.

for example, Memphis, Tennessee, which having had few buildings to begin with, have accomplished the destruction of the little they had.

Massachusetts' pioneering preservation campaign was waged in 1847. A group of private citizens in Deerfield attempted to preserve and move to another site the oldest house in town, the last remaining building which had even survived an Indian attack on the village in 1704. A broadside was printed, letters were written to the local paper, and solicitations were made to raise the sum of $400. Like New England's most famous subsequent early venture in preservation, the 1863 campaign to save the Hancock House in Boston, and like countless succeeding efforts, the Deerfield project was a failure. Not enough people cared; certainly not enough were willing to provide funds to prevent the destruction of an old landmark.

Some few tentative steps towards preservation were more successful. In 1850, New York State acquired, almost by accident, Washington's Headquarters, the Jonathan Hasbrouck House, at Newburgh. In 1856 the State of Tennessee purchased Andrew Jackson's home, The Hermitage. And in 1853, the first successful private nationwide preservation organization was formed. This was the Mount Vernon Ladies' Association, dedicated to the single-minded purpose of preserving and restoring the home of the Father of His Country.

The trumpet-call might be sounded for a few singular buildings. In general, the nineteenth-century response to the loss of the country's visual heritage was at most mildly elegiac. Change, newness, in a word, "progress" were accepted as synonyms for "better." A New Year's greeting issued to the customers of the Philadelphia *Public Ledger* in 1860 is typical. Oddly enough, the building shown, Latrobe's waterworks, must have been deeply impressed in the city's consciousness. When the greeting was issued it had been gone from the Philadelphia townscape for over 30 years. With a bow to the past, but faith in the future, the *Ledger* welcomed 1860:

> Yon Marble Hall — Irreverently Styled
> "The Pepperbox" — Was, Once, Our City's Pride;
> Around It, Lofty Trees and Verdure Smiled —
> Now Swept Away By Times Unsparing Tide.
> Alas! 'Tis Sad — With Every Fading Year —
> To See Our "Ancient Landmarks" Disappear!
>
> Increase of Population On the Banks
> Of Schuylkill Must the Waters Soon Pollute;
> Then Fairmount's Buildings, Mounds and
>   Rough-hewn Tanks
> Will Pass Away, Its Waterwheels Be Mute.
> Thus — Though Improvements Mark Each Changing Year,
> 'Tis Sad to See Old "Landmarks" Disappear.

Plus ça change, plus la même. The same sentiments, couched in less flowery terms perhaps, the same pious obeisance to familiar landmarks, open space, pure water can still be heard when the planning boards, the chambers of commerce and the booster clubs get together to discuss future growth. And the kicker's apt to be the same too. The amenities of the townscape are considered expendable in the name of "improvement" — for which read short-term economic gain.

For that matter, few preservationists in the late nineteenth century and the early years of the twentieth exhibited any interest in the quality of either the natural or the man-made environment. Patriotic societies, family associations, occasionally government agencies, focused on single buildings, pursuing aims more patriotic than aesthetic. They — and their successors who still constitute a strong force in the preservation movement — were ruled by what might be termed the George-Washington-Slept-Here syndrome. The buildings in which they were interested were those in which great men had lived or great events, preferably of the Revolutionary period, had transpired. These were to be preserved, and perhaps restored, so that the visitor to such sacred precincts might be infused, by some mysterious process of osmosis, with the patriotic virtues of former inhabitants.

No one would deny that these pioneering preservationists, often in the face of enormous obstacles, saved an important body of American buildings. But because their aims were narrow, and because nobody else had any aims at all, whole facets of the American cultural heritage began to disappear. By the end of the nineteenth century the urban Dutch buildings of New York City and Albany had vanished, along with most traces of Swedish colonization along the lower Delaware. Other reminders of the multiplicity of national strains woven into the fabric of American life were also being obliterated or severely decimated — the remnants of French settlements along the Mississippi, of the Spanish along the Gulf coast, the unique farmhouses developed by the Dutch on Long Island and in northern New Jersey.

Albany, New York, North Pearl Street, from Maiden Lane, early 1800's.

Delmas House, Pascagoula, Mississippi, 1780–1947.

If buildings other than those associated with heroic figures were not protected, it was probably because they simply weren't old enough to capture the public fancy. The appreciation of architecture operates under a grandfather clause, or perhaps it might be more accurate to say a great-grandfather clause. Aesthetically, the generation gap has been with us for a long time. We tend to denigrate the tastes of the generation or two immediately preceding our own at the same time that we are attracted to the life style of their predecessors, first, perhaps, as merely amusingly quaint, and then as the object of serious study and admiration. So Americans of the first half of the nineteenth century looked far beyond their own beginnings to the remote past of ancient Greece and Rome, of medieval Europe, even of Egypt for their models. The buildings of their own past were viewed with contempt as examples of crudity and bad taste. The mid-century attitude towards buildings of the eighteenth century, in other words, was not very different from that of Lewis Mumford in 1924, when he called those of the 1880's "disreputable." They were objects to be discarded, or, if not, in an era which was more conserving of materials and less bound by the cost of labor than ours, lost by "modernization" into a totally new form. Calvert Vaux' project, published in *Harper's New Monthly Magazine* in 1855, was only one of many contemporary schemes for transforming what he characterized as an "ugly . . . old-fashioned homestead" which could not "be contemplated by the rising generation with anything like satisfaction" into a country house which was at least tolerable according to mid-Victorian standards of taste and suitability.

Residence of Thomas Powell, Newburgh, New York, before alterations.

Residence of Thomas Powell, redesigned by Calvert Vaux.

The Philadelphia Centennial Exposition of 1876 introduced the average American to more than the wonders of the art of such far-off places as Japan or Turkey, or Norman Shaw's version of Tudor England. The celebration of a hundred years of national life embraced, however tentatively, the arts and artifacts of the colonial period as well as its political and military history. The Connecticut pavilion, according to one contemporary, was "intended to represent a colonial homestead of a generation ago," and displayed some examples of early Connecticut furniture. Even more fascinating to visitors was "The New England Farmer's Home" completed with hostesses in period costume, and furnished with authentic pieces.

The sparks ignited by the Centennial flickered fitfully sometimes, but never quite went out. The summer of 1877 was the occasion of a by now almost mythical walking tour in the course of which colonial buildings along New England's coast were sketched by a group of young architects, two of them on holiday from the drafting-room of Henry Hobson Richardson, the Messrs. McKim and White. In 1879 the American Institute of Architects appointed a committee to study colonial building practices. Over the next several decades the interest in colonial, Georgian and Federal buildings grew so intense that it sometimes posed a threat to the objects of its own admiration. No museum would become party to the vandalism involved in cutting a painting into six separate pieces so that the component parts might be viewed by a wider audience. But no such scruples afflicted some of the early devotees of the work of America's colonial architects and builders. Not only buildings scheduled for demolition, but those left standing were stripped of their paneling and other decorative detail. Houses such as Philadelphia's Stedman-Powel House (now beautifully restored on the exterior) and Stamper-Blackwell House were raped of their interiors, the former for installation in the Philadelphia Museum of Art and the American Wing of the Metropolitan Museum, the latter for Winterthur. It was a practice all too common among museum and private collectors in the 1920's and 30's.

If an excess of zeal was sometimes more damaging to early buildings than benign neglect, the burgeoning interest in the colonial period brought benefits as well. Its architecture and decorative arts became the object of serious study. One symbol of that strong interest was John D. Rockefeller, Jr.'s, decision, in 1926, to restore a large area of a colonial village. In so doing, he and his associates were confronted with the fruits of a century and a half of neglect of the country's architectural heritage. Even in an area as relatively undisturbed as Williamsburg, the sleepy, abandoned capital of colonial Virginia, buildings had gone whose loss, now that they were appreciated, was felt too keenly to be borne. The decision was made to rebuild.

Yet such a loss can never really be recouped. A reconstruction is not a fully adequate substitute for the original. It's as if the Louvre, having failed to recover the stolen Mona Lisa, had hung a good silkscreen print in its place and told the public that it was just as good as the real thing. At Williamsburg, where approximately half the buildings are reconstructions, one is constantly confronted with shadow and substance and the distinctions become blurred. There is, for example, the niggling question of what Capitol is it? Not, actually, the one in which Patrick Henry made his impassioned speech or George Mason introduced Virginia's Declaration of Rights. It is, rather, an earlier building, gutted by fire in 1747. The second Capitol, built on the foundations of the first, but in quite different form, had also been gone for almost a century when the reconstruction began. The earlier version was chosen, partly because it was more distinguished architecturally, partly because better documentary evidence of its original appearance was available.

Even in so ambitious a program as Williamsburg's the aims remained narrow. Besides preserving the "beauty and charm of the old buildings and gardens of the city," Mr. Rockefeller saw Williamsburg as valuable for "the lesson it teaches of the patriotism,

The Bodleian Plate, engraved c. 1740 for an English publication that was never issued; discovered by Williamsburg researchers in the Bodleian Library at Oxford. It served as the basis for the restoration and reconstruction of several of the town's important buildings.

high purpose, and unselfish devotion of our forefathers to the common good." What Williamsburg presents is upper-class WASP history. The streets are clean; the slave cabins and outhouses have been suppressed. It is history without depth and without continuity. The clock has stopped and the past has been enshrined behind glass. And having put history in its niche, one can admire it and forget it. There is no spillover of history or art as a living presence able to enrich our daily lives. At the same time that Rockefeller money from one hand was saving Williamsburg, funds from the other were accomplishing the work of destruction. In the 1930's the Standard Oil Company erected a gas station on the site of Charleston's Gabriel Manigault House. The station bears a plaque which reads: "In order to preserve the architectural traditions of Charleston, the brickwork and woodwork of the demolished Gabriel Manigault House 1800 AD were used in this station."

Manigault-Gibbes House, Charleston, South Carolina, c. 1800–c. 1930.

This is not to single out Williamsburg and/or the Rockefellers for censure. Certainly Williamsburg and the museum villages that followed it have performed two services that cannot be too highly valued. Their research departments have become centers for the collection and dissemination of knowledge on the identification, care, and restoration of the materials of the past. And by presenting that past in tangible and dramatic form, they have aroused admiration for at least certain aspects of the nation's heritage. What Williamsburg does exemplify and epitomize are American attitudes towards that heritage. By the end of World War II, after nearly a century of preservation effort, those attitudes were well-established. The remaining great public monuments and stately mansions of the eighteenth and early nineteenth century were virtually exempt from destruction. The rest was fair game.

The situation began to assume crisis proportions in the post-war years. In the 1930's, the Historic American Buildings Survey had been established to record the country's architectural patrimony. By the early 1960's, some 20 to 25 per cent of the buildings listed had been destroyed or seriously altered. And the HABS had concentrated on buildings prior to 1830. Nobody was counting the numerically far greater losses among late nineteenth and early twentieth-century buildings.

Wetter House, Savannah, Georgia, an early nineteenth-century house, embellished in 1857 with cast iron ornament featuring plaques adorned with portraits of poets. Recorded by HABS in 1936, it was destroyed shortly thereafter.

The acceleration of loss was, in large part, an unintentional byblow of Federal programs planned, ironically, to improve the country's quality of life. After a decade of depression and half a decade of war there was a pent-up need for roads, schools, housing, factories, in short, for construction of all kinds. A series of bills provided both public funds and aid to private industry in fulfilling those needs. There were, in sum, not millions, but billions for new construction and destruction to make way for it, and only pennies for the protection of the man-made environment.

II

The whittling away of the amenities of our surroundings has been going on for a long time in America. Its causes are various; taken together, they make a sorry tale of indifference, ignorance, greed, and downright criminality.

There are, of course, the unavoidable losses, determined by the hand of God. Storm and flood, earthquake and accidental fire have all taken their toll, although it is a relatively small one in comparison to man-made destruction. And hurricanes, tornadoes and tremors have no bias for or against historic structures. These are the only true accidental losses and, perhaps, therefore, less shadowed with tragedy than those where man has been the agent

Trinity Church, Episcopal, Pass Christian, Mississippi, 1850–1969. Destroyed by hurricane "Camille."

Forks of Cypress, Lauderdale County, Alabama, burned to ground after being struck by lightning.

Ossian Hall, Fairfax County, Virginia, 1783–1959.

André Breton watercolor, house at Francisville, Pennsylvania, burned by the British during the Revolution.

Resurrection Manor, St. Mary's County, Maryland.

of destruction. Yet there are areas — in the Carolinas, and along the Jersey, Long Island, New England and Gulf coasts — where the scars of past storms are not forgotten.

Fire is a more complicated agent of destruction. The great urban conflagrations like those that leveled vast areas of Chicago and Boston in the 1870's are hopefully a phenomenon of the past thanks to modern firefighting and fireproofing methods. Old buildings, however, with their dry and seasoned timbers, remain particularly vulnerable to fire, especially those in isolated areas where help is far away. So each year adds to the roster of loss a quota of Southern plantation houses and New England seaside hotels.

These, like the losses from nature's buffeting, may be mourned but are somehow acceptable. But the repeated tale of arson is not. "Burned by local teenagers," "fire of mysterious origin," "burned while vacant awaiting restoration," "fire department said fire had been set." Sometimes the stories would be funny if they weren't so sad. Several years ago, in Fairfax County, Virginia, the local volunteer firemen held one of those house-burnings-for-practice in which suburban and rural fire departments indulge every so often. The target for this particular exercise was Ossian Hall. True, the house had been sold to a developer and ravaged by vandals before being put to the torch. The funny part? Annandale Fire Co. #23, in fine, traditional form, carries an emblem on its fire trucks. And the emblem? Ossian Hall.

Man's violence also accounts for losses in war. America has been lucky. We have never had a Coventry, a Rotterdam or a Cologne. The damage done to Washington in the War of 1812 was soon repaired. And even the losses in Charleston, Atlanta, Richmond and other parts of the South during the Civil War shrink to insignificance beside the magnitude of loss incurred through totally senseless destruction and negligent disdain of our heritage.

Neglect, indifference, apathy, private and public, have accounted for the decay and eventual total ruin of whole cities of buildings. Sometimes genuine economic hardship on the part of the private owners is involved. And as long as we fail to recognize a public responsibility for preservation of the most important of these buildings, there is no recourse. Resurrection Manor in St. Mary's County, Maryland, one of the last fully documented examples of a relatively unaltered small seventeenth-century house (its "great room" was built in 1642/3, a second room added in 1654), is in far worse condition today than it was when the accompanying photograph was taken. Uncared for, it is doomed to collapse as others cited in this book already have.

Sometimes, of course, neglect may be less damaging than the wrong kind of attention. A preservation expert once remarked that the aesthetic value of more old buildings had been destroyed by the application of asbestos shingles than by any other cause. Other ill-conceived alterations can be equally harmful. One of the most handsome early nineteenth-century facades in Ohio, that of Hudson's Baldwin-Buss House, has been severely, although fortunately not irreparably, damaged by the addition of a tacky porch and crudely proportioned dormers.

To the sins of sloth and ignorance might be added that of pride. Some of the most ardent and eloquent advocates of preservation are architects willing to adapt their own designs to complement existing older structures. Other practitioners consider the retention of such buildings as interference with their creative prerogatives. An architect in Princeton, New Jersey, with a more than local reputation as a designer of Neo-Colonial houses, once argued before the town's planning board that a Victorian mansion in the center of a proposed housing development should be demolished. Although a financially attractive offer for the house and sufficient land to provide it with ample grounds had been made to the developer, the architect claimed that its very presence would be detrimental to his conception of a Williamsburg - style community. His clinching argument was that his plan provided for gaslit streets — on reflection a feature rather more compatible with the age of Victoria than that of Patrick Henry. Logic had little to do with the case in any event. The planners had no legal powers to stay demolition. The house was razed. The developer eventually chose another architect and there were neither gaslights nor Williamsburg - style houses.

A similar situation in Richmond, Virginia, this time attracting interest on a national scale, has had an equally unhappy conclusion. The First and Merchants National Bank is going ahead with plans to demolish five iron front buildings on the city's Main Street. Pleas to retain them which even included architect's renderings showing how the iron fronts could be incorporated into the bank's proposed office complex, were rejected. The bank has offered what it considers a satisfactory compromise — parts of the ironwork will be dismantled and stored in Richmond's Valentine Museum, the office pavilion that replaces the iron fronts will be only four stories high, in keeping with the scale of other buildings on the street. But the design will be that of the bank's chosen architect, which the bank, and presumably the architect, feels to be a more valuable asset than a significant portion of Richmond's heritage.

The economics of preservation, or to look at the other side of the coin, destruction, is riddled with paradox. Sometimes a little judicious poverty is the best friend of old buildings. Whole areas in such places as Savannah and Nantucket were saved for a generation that would appreciate them because the economic dislocations following the Civil War in one case and the demise of whaling in the other made their replacement impossible. Complete economic collapse, of course, condemns buildings as well as their owners to ruin. The Williams - Macon House is only one of several once gracious plantation houses in Halifax County, North Carolina, long abandoned and now ruinous. Its fate is echoed in other long - depressed agricultural areas as well as in the textile mill towns of New England.

With shifting economic values the newly affluent area may suffer as much, in aesthetic and environmental terms, as the impoverished one. Fairfax County, Virginia, just across the Potomac from Washington, was, for over two hundred years, a relatively stable rural community. In the quarter century after World War II the county changed at an exponential rate to one in which suburban housing tracts and industrial parks linked by major highways set the patterns of land use. The economic advantages of the change may be obvious, but the county acquired concomitant problems, among them the disappearance of valued landmarks. One of these was Maplewood, an anomaly in Northern Virginia, its only domestic monument, built in the locally - depressed days after the Civil War, in the flamboyant Second Empire style. In 1962 Maplewood became the property of the Westgate Corporation, developers of an industrial and research complex. It served as the corporation's temporary headquarters until it was rapidly, and unexpectedly, demolished in 1970.

Shifting patterns of land use and alterations in neighborhoods are nothing new. Ever since the advent of the railroad and

Baldwin-Buss House, Hudson, Ohio, in original state.

Baldwin-Buss House, after alteration.

Iron Front Buildings, Main Street, Richmond, Virginia, soon to be replaced by a modern office building.

Williams-Macon House, Airlie, Halifax County, North Carolina. A fine Federal house, built around 1800, and closely related to contemporary houses in Virginia.

Maplewood, Fairfax County, Virginia, 1870–1970.

Port Royal, Frankford, Pennsylvania, 1762–c.1940; photograph taken c. 1900.

Port Royal in 1937.

Eighteenth and early nineteenth-century row houses, St. James Street, Philadelphia.

the streetcar made some form of commuting possible there has been a geographic gap between our prime commercial and residential areas. The automobile made the gap wider and more extensive. The void between the two has often been filled by the meanest and least attractive of uses — the used car lot, the second hand store, the plastic hamburger stand, the drive-in movie, in short, the whole panoply of strip city. And woe betide the landmark caught in that no man's land. Port Royal, built in 1762 in Frankford, Pennsylvania, was one of the most grandiose and elegant of the Georgian mansions in the Philadelphia environs. By 1900, fashionable Philadelphia had moved out along the Main Line and Port Royal, though still intact in a semi-rural setting, was dilapidated. Some forty years later the neighborhood had become dingily commercial. Port Royal's interiors went to Winterthur, but nobody wanted the house itself in those surroundings. It was demolished.

The deterioration of neighborhoods has been generously assisted by heedless tax policies that in the long run benefit no one but the real estate speculator out for short term profit. The property owner who improves, maintains and repairs buildings is penalized by higher assessments. Conversely, the one who allows his buildings to deteriorate, enjoys the benefit of lower taxes. He can, in many cases, reduce his expenses even further by clearing the land of buildings and holding it for an expected rise in values.

When the downward spiral has created an eyesore compounded of crumbling buildings and vacant lots one solution has been for the government to step in and attempt to revitalize the area. Until very recently, unfortunately, many urban renewal projects have involved total clearance of often enormous sites. Little thought has been given to the rehabilitation of potentially viable older buildings that might provide a link between the reclaimed area and its roots in the urban scene. Even in so vaunted a project as Philadelphia's Society Hill, rows of eighteenth and nineteenth-century houses were destroyed to provide a site for a pair of high-rise towers, the density of occupancy being considered necessary to make the area a financial success. Ironically, the restored areas of Society Hill have proved so popular that ever rising property values threaten to jeopardize the project's initial purpose of luring the middle class back to the city. The towers were, therefore, perhaps not necessary. They are handsome buildings, designed by I. M. Pei, but they are overwhelmingly out of scale with the rest of the neighborhood and stand nakedly, surrounded by what looks like nothing so much as a bombed-out heath, in contrast to the close-packed rows of townhouses on the nearby streets.

Urban renewal is only one of the major programs that has resulted in mass destruction in the name of progress. Perhaps even more damaging has been the incredible amount of destruction and construction, most of it heavily subsidized by the Federal government, undertaken on behalf of the automobile. It would certainly be unrealistic to think that cars can be wished away, but the dislocations caused by highway construction in rural and urban areas alike must be minimized. There is something seriously wrong with our planning when reports from cities and towns all over the eastern part of the country describe almost half their lost landmarks as replaced by parking lots. We have been trading our heritage for a mass of asphalt.

III

This is a sad book. It is meant to be. It represents only a small sample of the rich and diverse delights that have vanished from the

American scene. Some were major monuments. Some were examples of interesting types, illuminating the contributions made to American life by differing cultures and disciplines. Some were buildings of no particular architectual distinction, but were deeply woven into the fabric of their communities. Not all of them, on sober reflection, could have been or should have been saved. But far too many, even of the minor structures, were destroyed heedlessly, for insufficient reasons, and were replaced with structures or, in the case of parking spaces and vacant lots, nonstructures that have diminished the quality of the man - made environment.

Taken in sum, they illuminate those intangible losses that far outstrip the physical loss of any single structure. We have lost, or at best gravely diminished, the variety and excitement that once characterized much of American culture. The differences in racial, national and regional preferences that once transmuted even nationally - accepted styles into something individual and locally unique is gone. In place of E Pluribus Unum, a unity woven out of pluralism, our landscape is becoming homogenized. Americans flock in ever - increasing numbers to Europe to gaze in admiration at Paris, London and Rome. Part of what they are seeking for is what we are destroying in our own environment — the variety and sense of continuity that come from preserving links with the national past.

In erasing diversity we have also been destroying the sense of identity that is immediately transmitted through readily recognizable objects. It was once possible to tell at a glance that you were in a New England village or a mid - Atlantic city like Philadelphia or Baltimore, or a Midwestern town of broad, tree - lined streets. It is still possible to feel this sense of place, but it is becoming a rarer experience. The entrance to our towns, and the skylines of our cities, glimpsed from the window of car or train, look very much alike.

We are losing not only identity in place, but in time. The buildings that have gone and the ones that are threatened constitute a valuable historic and artistic testimonial, recorded in brick and mortar rather than in ink, of what America has been and what it is becoming. We need our old buildings as a point of reference, not just to tell us about the past, but to help place the present and future in perspective.

And perhaps we need some of them, most of all, for the soul - nourishing beauty they can provide. A young Puerto Rican girl from New York's Lower East Side in a composition published recently in a book entitled *Can't You Hear Me Talking to You?* writes: "I look at my block like a tapestry of dull colors that you see every day, a tapestry that never ends. The block I live on looks like a jungle, but instead of having trees and animals on it, there are ugly buildings big and small." The yearning for beauty is obviously not just the prerogative of the comfortable suburban upper middle class.

On the other hand, it must be recognized that preservation is no panacea for the ills of our society and that sometimes it may interfere with the pursuit of a better life. The rehabilitation of deteriorated city areas has, in the past, often meant the dislocation of tenants and property owners who have no place to go but to another deteriorating area. The mills of the great post - Civil War industrial expansion may be fascinating to students of engineering and planning practices. To those who have worked in and lived with them they show a different face. A lawyer in Manchester, New Hampshire, asked when that town would stop destroying the buildings of the Amoskeag mill complex, replied, "Not as long as any-

India Wharf, Boston, c. 1805–1962, Charles Bulfinch. The only remaining Bulfinch commercial building in Boston was torn down to provide temporary parking space during a redevelopment project on the waterfront.

Kensington, Richmond County, South Carolina, 1851/3. An unusual plantation house, melding the luxurious forms of the Second Empire into what is basically a South Carolina wooden farmhouse. Kensington is doomed to destruction by vandals and weather unless action is taken soon.

body's alive who ever had to work in them." Obviously for Manchester there is no room for admiration of architectural quality beneath the searing memory of filth, bad lighting and indifferent ventilation.

And yet, although it is clear that not all buildings can, or even should be saved, we are beginning to understand that the frontier is closed and we are going to have to live with what we've got. Preservation does not mean an end to change and progress. It does mean the imposition of certain conditions on the process of change.

There is certainly ample precedent for shaping our development. The growth of suburbs was not only encouraged, but heavily subsidized, through low-cost FHA and VA loans and Federal tax laws. Local zoning and taxes, private and public financial policies all tended to bypass the old in favor of the new, no matter what the relative merits of the two.

There are encouraging signs of new approaches to redress the balance. A number of communities, large and small — Providence, Boston, Cape May — to name just a few, have followed the example of the pioneers — Charleston and New Orleans — in extending the protection of special zoning to historic districts. The validity of such laws was upheld by the United States Supreme Court in the case of Berman vs. Parker, decided in 1954. The Justices ruled that "It is within the power of the legislature to determine that the community should be beautiful as well as healthy, spacious as well as clean, well-balanced as well as carefully patrolled."

Zoning, of course, is not a cure-all. Other avenues now being explored hold equal and in some situations greater promise. Various forms of easements can protect the appearance of historic buildings and areas while allowing great flexibility in use. Arrangements involving the transfer of development and air rights from historic buildings to surrounding properties offer potentially attractive solutions, especially in our larger cities. Private financial institutions are beginning to look with more favor on loans for restoration and rehabilitation in the light of the cold, hard, financial success of such areas as Georgetown and Society Hill.

On the national level, a number of important steps have been taken. The National Trust for Historic Preservation continues to enlarge its program of education, advice and consultation for local groups. It also dispenses privately-funded grants to assist such groups undertaking feasibility studies on the preservation and adaptation of worthy buildings to new uses. The National Historic Preservation Act of 1966 grants some measure of protection from encroachment by Federally-funded projects on those sites deemed worthy of inclusion in the National Register of Historic Places. And the establishment of the Register has provided a national mechanism for the assessment of the nation's cultural property.

Yet these are just beginnings, hopeful signs of a burgeoning interest in our architectural heritage. Meanwhile the fight goes on city by city, building by building, to save what is left until the new programs become effective. For although the values of preservation have gained some acceptance, this is by no means universal. Time is both friend and enemy. Given enough it seems likely that public attitudes will change. But the important thing is judicious restraint now. The decision to destroy is irreversible.

Meanwhile the assessment of our patrimony must continue, especially the reevaluation of our not-so-distant past. This book,

Heck-Andrews House, Raleigh, North Carolina, 1870. Once Blount Street was Raleigh's most elegant section. Now its remaining fine homes are threatened by the rapid expansion of State office buildings and their accompanying parking lots.

in attempting to review what we have already lost, may hopefully provide some guidelines for the future. It represents only the briefest selection from the thousands of worthy buildings that have been lost. Whole volumes of the same size could be compiled on Philadelphia or Boston or Chicago or Cleveland. One has been done on New York. An attempt has been made to include not just the great monuments of the past, but the smaller and perhaps less signficant structures which had local meaning. The purpose has been to review to only a slight extent the losses of the distant past, concentrating instead on those of the last thirty years. The record is far from complete. It is based on information from areas where people care about what is happening to their communities. In too many other places, nobody's even keeping score.

going, going , . . .

AMOSKEAG MANUFACTURING COMPANY   Manchester, New Hampshire. 1838–. As the mill complex appeared in 1967 before the canals were filled and partial demolition begun.

14

gone

NATIONAL PRESBYTERIAN CHURCH   Washington, D.C., 1889 – 1965, J. C. Cady.

16

LOST AMERICA

From the Atlantic to the Mississippi

I. Civic Pride

American government buildings are erected — and destroyed — not by fiat, but at the direction of our elected representatives. They are, in fact, the property of the people who, after all, pay for them. As such, they are the single most cogent expression of who we are, what our aspirations are, how we visualize ourselves. We have no stronger collective symbols. If you see a picture of the dome of the United States Capitol, its message is immediately clear. The place is Washington; the building is the seat and center of the American government.

Perhaps it is the strength of such buildings as symbols that accounts for the preservation of so many of the major ones. Approximately half the state houses east of the Mississippi are over one hundred years old. But the force of that symbolism often fails to rub off on lesser public buildings, many of them of greater architectural distinction. A city councilman might shudder if he heard the Capitol was going to be torn down, but he will vote without a qualm to raze the old city hall and build a new one. He will have little regard for the relative quality of what will be lost and what will be gained, and the chances are that the quality will not be as good. Through the third quarter of the nineteenth century, public commissions went to the country's leading architects. Starting with the competitions for the Capitol and New York's City Hall, on to the Bulfinch state houses for Massachusetts, Maine and Connecticut, up to Henry Hobson Richardson's county courthouses in Springfield, Mass., (threatened with demolition) and Pittsburgh, there was a clearcut attempt to get the best. And then things fell apart. Nobody ever asked either Louis Sullivan or Frank Lloyd Wright to design a major government building. And until very recently the Architect of the Capitol, responsible for an addition which defaced the East Front and cost the public $24½ million dollars, wasn't even an architect.

The fault is all of ours. If as citizens we value efficient office cubicles and inefficient but cheap parking arrangements over an expression of the majesty and dignity of our form of government, we will get what we deserve.

1. HENDERSON COUNTY COURTHOUSE Henderson, Kentucky, 1834 – 1964, Littleberry Weaver. The building served as headquarters and hospital during the Civil War. Not even the handsome cupola was saved from demolition one hundred years later.

2. OLD COURTHOUSE Zanesville, Ohio, 1809 – 1874, James Hampson. Early Ohio buildings were often strongly reminiscent of the eastern areas where the territory's first settlers had their roots. Hampson was a Virginian, and the courthouse clearly reflects his origins. It served as the State House until the capital moved to Chillicothe in 1812. The Zanesville building then became the Muskingum County courthouse, acquiring, in 1833, two wings which housed offices and an atheneum. Demolished.

3. FIRST COURTHOUSE AND JAIL Cumberland, Maryland, 1797 – 1966. With its sturdy high stone basement to house the jail, and a more elegant brick superstructure to accommodate the court, this building remained a useful resource of the community for many years. An Italianate attic was added in the mid-nineteenth century. Although structurally sound, it was razed to make way for an annex to the town's library. Cumberland has lost many of its fine early and mid-nineteenth century buildings in recent years, despite the vigorous protests of local taxpayers. The town is now threatened with the loss of its one registered National Landmark — the Queen City Hotel and Station (1871 / 72 – ?).

With Jefferson's Virginia State Capitol at Richmond and the United States Capitol as precedents, versions of the Classic Revival became an almost official style for early nineteenth-century public buildings. The majestic structures erected in this style as capitols in Maine, Connecticut, North Carolina, Tennessee and other states survive, although some have been converted to new uses. The smaller local courthouses were usually built in simple, temple form, not readily adaptable to addition or conversion. Most of them have already gone; the remainder are rapidly disappearing.

4. OLD COURTHOUSE Portsmouth, New Hampshire, 1836–1952. A small structure, deriving considerable monumentality from its simplified Doric portico, the courthouse was erected on the site of a yet older building, the almshouse of 1755. In 1919 it was moved to a different site to make room for a fire station. Ironically, the building burned on its new site and had to be totally demolished.

5. MADISON COUNTY COURTHOUSE Huntsville, Alabama, 1837/40 – 1914, George Steele. Designed in emulation of the Parthenon, this was a dignified building, despite the somewhat overpowering dome and too-delicate cupola. It was still structurally sound when razed.

6. TOWN HALL Waukesha, Wisconsin, c. 1842 – 1970. While newer styles were becoming fashionable in the East, the westward movement carried simplified forms of the Greek Revival with it. This tidy, unpretentious example was lost when funds to move and restore it could not be raised.

8. PHILADELPHIA COUNTY PRISON   Moyamensing, Pennsylvania, 1829–1968; 7. DEBTORS' PRISON, 1832–1968; Thomas U. Walter. For his first important commission, the architect, later responsible for the dome of the United States Capitol, chose a sturdy, but highly imaginative version of castellated "Gothick." Its romantic quality is clearly conveyed in his own painting of the building. The Debtors' Prison, an unusually early but somewhat heavy-handed essay in the Egyptian mode, suggests that debt may have been considered a worse crime than felony. Actually, the building never housed debtors, imprisonment for debt having been abolished in Pennsylvania by the time of its completion. The use of Egyptian forms for a prison seems to have been accepted as suitable. John Haviland used the style, with far more assurance and freedom, in his prison for New York City. The building, metaphorically known as "The Tombs," built in 1836–38, is also gone. His New Jersey State Penitentiary, built at about the same time, is still in use at Trenton.

9. ESSEX COUNTY COURTHOUSE Newark, New Jersey, 1838–1906, John Haviland. The Egyptian Revival was never very popular. Examples were always rare, and have become rarer. Regret over the loss of this structure, with its Italianate addition of a decade later, may be tempered by appreciation for the quality of its replacment. The present Beaux-Arts Classic building by Cass Gilbert is seen rising in the background of the photograph.

10. CITY HALL Utica, New York, 1852/3–1968, Richard M. Upjohn. Upjohn, probably best known for his Gothic churches, preferred other styles for secular commissions. The Italianate forms and the simple, powerful cupola used here may reflect his Italian travels. The building was demolished as part of an urban renewal project.

11. THIRD ONONDAGA COUNTY COURTHOUSE Syracuse, New York,
1856/57 – 1968, Horatio Nelson White. A landmark in every sense of
the word, this Anglo-Norman structure was an important adornment of
the Syracuse townscape. Despite the advocacy of members of the
Department of Architecture at Syracuse University who drew up plans
for its potential rehabilitation for community use, the building was
demolished. In a futile bow to its champions, the tower was disassembled
and stored for possible erection in a city park.

In the mid-nineteenth century a succession of architects—Ammi B. Young, Isaiah Rogers, Alfred B. Mullett and William A. Potter—held the title of Supervising Architect of the United States Treasury Department. Under their supervision, customs houses, courthouses, post offices and other Federal buildings were designed in Washington for erection in all parts of the country. Taken in sum, their production may appear to bear the twin stigmata of bureaucratic architecture—routine design and monotony in detail. Individually, many were handsome and dignified buildings. In smaller cities and towns they were often the only structures designed by competent professional architects. They introduced the latest in fashionable styles from the urban centers of the eastern seaboard, as well as the advances of a rapidly expanding building technology.

12. FEDERAL BUILDING   Indianapolis, Indiana, c. 1857—1963, Ammi B. Young. The building was sold to a bank in 1906. After its demolition, a larger commercial building was erected on the site.

13. UNITED STATES CUSTOM HOUSE Mobile, Alabama, 1852/4 — 1963, Ammi B. Young. The Renaissance Revival style, introduced to England by Sir Charles Barry and to the United States by John Notman in the Philadelphia Atheneum of 1845/7, was accepted with enthusiasm by Young as a dignified alternative, still within a classical framework, to the waning Greek Revival.

15. UNITED STATES CUSTOMS HOUSE Detroit,
Michigan, 1855/6 — 1964, Ammi B. Young.

14. Detail, interior, cast iron staircase.

16. POST OFFICE AND COURTHOUSE   Portland, Maine,
1868/71 — 1965, Alfred B. Mullett. Built to replace an
earlier courthouse by Young burned in the great Portland
fire of 1866. The solid and elegantly subdued Renaissance
Revival design was not unusual for Mullett. He is better
known, however, for such flamboyant "General Grant"
buildings as the recently restored State, War and Navy
Building in Washington or the demolished City Hall Post
Office in New York City. The site of the Portland building
is· now used as a parking lot.

17. SECOND CITY HALL
Pittsburgh, Pennsylvania,
1868 / 70 – 1953, Joseph W. Kerr.
A fine, restrained Second Empire
building with broadly proportioned
Italianate detailing. It was razed to make
way for a commercial building.

18. CITY MARKET Savannah, Georgia, 1870/2 — early 1950's, Scwaab and Muller. Municipal markets were once a common feature of the urban scene. Savannah's, with its repeated sweeping gables, was an especially attractive example of the species.

31

19. MARION COUNTY COURTHOUSE Indianapolis, Indiana, 1876–1962, Isaac Hodgson. Obviously nothing was too good for the county fathers. The 1876 Courthouse had everything — statuary, carved cartouches, elaborate iron crestings and finials. It was a notable expression of the exuberant optimism of the centennial year. Although the massing of the architectural elements was less sophisticated than those used in Detroit's City Hall (fig. 20), the building's rich contrasts of texture and light and shade had great visual impact. It was replaced by a new City-County Building.

20. CITY HALL   Detroit, Michigan, 1871–1961, James Anderson. The vigor and bold plasticity of the Second Empire were most effective when organized in a rational and well-ordered composition of clearly defined pavilions. This was the case in Detroit's City Hall, a handsome and dignified contribution to the city's townscape.

21. CITY HALL   Grand Rapids, Michigan, 1888–1966, Elijah E. Myers. This substantially-built structure was distinguished by the careful detailing of its stonework. The high quality of Victorian craftsmanship was also displayed on the interior with its monumental cast iron staircase and ornamental polychrome tile floors. The picturesque tower, with its corbeled clock, was a grace note on the Grand Rapids skyline. The building was razed as part of an urban renewal project.

Utilizing the whole repertoire of styles popular in the second half of the nineteenth century, local builders and architects turned out minor public buildings that suited the eclectic tastes of their clients. The results were not always very good architecture, but the towering city hall or county courthouse was often the dominating and identifying landmark in small-town America.

23. COURTHOUSE   Arlington, Virginia, 1898—1960, A. Goenner. The tower was removed in the course of a complete rebuilding of the courthouse.

22. LAKE COUNTY COURTHOUSE   Waukegan, Illinois, 1878—1967. This made way for a modern ten-story office building and adjoining court complex.

24. ESCAMBIA COUNTY COURTHOUSE   Pensacola, Florida, 1885 – c. 1938.   The neo-Georgian clock seems an odd and charming touch in Florida.   The county traded the site to the Federal government for erection of a new post office.

25. BERRIEN COUNTY COURTHOUSE   St. Joseph, Michigan, 1895. Bell tower demolished 1959.   The artist who sketched the courthouse a few months before its appearance was drastically altered by demolition of the bell tower recalls: ". . . not particularly distinctive, but it was St. Joe's landmark for generations.   For 17 years it was always twenty-five minutes past eleven in St. Joe, when the old clock was stopped . . . . in my childhood how we loved to climb the winding stairs to see the high glimpse of Lake Michigan and surrounding country."

COURTHOUSES I HAVE SEEN - NO. 19 - ST. JOSEPH, MICH. (BERRIEN CO.)
1895

26. UNITED STATES POST OFFICE (later St. Raphael High School)   Springfield, Ohio, c. 1888–1970. The strong geometric forms and bold stonework that characterized Richardsonian Romanesque were handled with varying degrees of success in the 1880's and 90's. This was one of the better ones. The site is now a parking lot for St. Raphael's Church.

II. Faith, Hope & Charity

It might be assumed that those institutions charged with preserving the culture of the past and transmitting it to future generations would be in the forefront of historic and architectural preservation. Don't count on it. Books are carefully tended by librarians; paintings and sculpture become the charge of curators. But frequently the fate of buildings is up to the real estate department. And so, decisions affecting them are too often made in terms of strict property values, without any consideration of aesthetic or cultural factors entering into the equation.

It's not usually Old Main that's in danger, although it's not always safe either. Colby College, in Waterville, Maine, demolished its 1867 Memorial Hall in 1962. The really vulnerable structures are those owned by universities, churches, charitable institutions, and, yes, even historical societies, that are only peripherally related to the institution's direct activities. There are a number of examples in other sections of this book that fall into that category — the Watson House, destroyed by Brown University (along with a fine Greek Revival mansion by Russell Warren); the Wyman Villa, torn down by Johns Hopkins; the outstanding nineteenth - century commercial buildings razed by the National Park Service in Philadelphia. The list could be a great deal longer. It might include the Sheffield and Noah Webster houses, owned by Yale, the one razed, the other rescued by Greenfield Village; the Federal Row in Baltimore, destroyed by the Maryland Historical Society for an addition to its headquarters; New York's Washington Square, a victim of both New York University and the Seamen's Church Institute.

There is hope. These institutions are especially dependent on their constituents — alumni, donors, members. If they demand that structures of real aesthetic and historical value be identified and maintained, the institutions will have to respond.

27. FIRST PRESBYTERIAN CHURCH (also known as Whalers' Church) Sag Harbor, Long Island, New York, 1844 —, tower destroyed 1938, attributed to Minard Lafever. The church might be described as highly refined Carpenter's Egyptian, a translation into wood of forms more usually executed in stone. The tower, however, utilized Greek motifs, freely imagined and of great elegance. It rose in tier upon tier of dazzling confectionery until struck down by the hurricane of 1938. It has never been replaced.

28. MORAVIAN CHURCH AND SCHOOL HOUSE Oley, Pennsylvania, 1743/5—1950's. A rare example of the survival of medieval half-timbered building types in America. Abandoned by the Moravians, who left Oley in 1765, it was converted to domestic use. Abandoned again, it slowly disintegrated and finally collapsed. The site is now an empty field.

29. ELDER BALLOU MEETING HOUSE   Cumberland, Rhode Island, 1740/49 — c. 1950. A notable, and unaltered surviving example of an early colonial meeting house, still preserving its medieval character in details of design and construction. Only the plastered ceiling and pitched roof suggested that this was an eighteenth, rather than a seventeenth - century building. Burned to the ground.

30. CHURCH OF PRINCE WILLIAM'S PARISH (also known as the Ruins of Sheldon) near Beaufort, South Carolina, 1745/55—1865. Lightning isn't supposed to strike twice, but one of America's most romantic ruins has been the double victim of violence. It was burned by the British in 1779. Rebuilt in 1826, it was burned by Union troops, and has never been restored.

31. CONGREGATIONAL CHURCH   Pittsfield, Massachusetts, 1789/93 — 1936, Charles Bulfinch. New England has lost a number of Bulfinch churches, of which the Pittsfield building was not one of the best. But it provides a fine case history of the fate of a church abandoned by its congregation. In 1851 there was a fire; the cupola was lost, and the congregation decided to build anew rather than attempt a restoration. The building was moved to the Maplewood School where it became first a gym and then a ballroom, gradually falling into disrepair. In 1930 an effort was made to raise funds to restore the building and move it to a site adjoining the Peace Party House (*see* fig. 67). It failed, probably due to the economic pressures of the Depression.

32. ORPHANS' CHAPEL   Charleston, South Carolina, 1802–1953, Gabriel Manigault. A small, but unusually monumental building for Charleston's most noted practitioner in the Federal style. It was demolished by a large mail-order firm for a parking lot at a time when Charleston preservationists were seeking alternate solutions.

33. FIRST PRESBYTERIAN CHURCH   Baltimore, Maryland, 1789–1854, towers added 1795, James Mosher and John Dalrymple. This was Baltimore's most impressive church of the period, so much so that Talbot Hamlin succumbed to the temptation to attribute it to Maximilien Godefroy, rather than two local builder-architects. The site was sold to the Federal government for a post office.

34. MORMON TEMPLE   Nauvoo, Illinois, 1841/5—1848. In 1841 Joseph Smith announced to his followers that the temple was to be built according to a revelation from God. Even after the prophet's murder in 1844 made the westward trek to Utah inevitable, work on the temple continued. Contemporaries often described its style as "Egyptian," but to modern eyes it looks rather like a strange cross between overblown New England meetinghouse and Neo-Classic monument. In any event, Joseph Smith, or the divine Word, must be credited, like Benjamin Henry Latrobe who created the famed corncob columns of the United States Capitol, with the invention of a new American architectural order. The colossal pilasters, with their "moonstone" bases and "sunstone" capitals, represented two of the three levels of heavenly glory in Mormon belief; the third was symbolized by the five-pointed stars in the cornice. In 1848, two years after most of the Mormons followed Brigham Young westward from Nauvoo, "Gentiles" put the temple to the torch. Although the walls still stood, a tornado in 1850 reduced them to a picturesque ruin. They were finally taken down as a menace to safety. The Historic Nauvoo Foundation plans to restore the temple, not completely, but to its ruinous state.

35. SCHOOL FOR THE BLIND   Louisville, Kentucky, 1856–1967, Francis Costigan. The Greek Revival retained its vigor in the
Midwest, South and Border States up to the time of the Civil War, although Greek detail was combined here with Roman
and Italianate motifs. The Costigan building was demolished despite inclusion in the National Register of Historic Places.

36. SCHOOL HOUSE Prescott, Massachusetts, 1813—1937. With the rise of free public education in the early nineteenth century, the little red school house became a salient feature of the rural American landscape. The buildings were usually simple vernacular structures often, like this one, possessed of a straightforward charm. In any case, they were evocative of a simpler era, and are fast disappearing with it.

37. AMERICAN ANTIQUARIAN SOCIETY Worcester Massachusetts, 1819 – c. 1910. Like many other early buildings for public and institutional use, this was a somewhat enlarged version of contemporary residential design. After the American Antiquarian Society moved to its second building, the first housed the Worcester Academy until its demolition.

38. COURTHOUSE Worcester, Massachusetts, 1801 – 1898, Charles Bulfinch; AMERICAN ANTIQUARIAN SOCIETY, 1853 – c. 1890, Thomas A. Tefft. Worcester's third courthouse was refurbished with an Italianate front in 1857, perhaps to complement the Antiquarian Society's second home. For an exhibition assembled for the Worcester Art Museum in 1838 Henry - Russell Hitchcock characterized the latter building as ". . . one of the best examples in America . . ." of the simple sort of renaissance design. Of the 74 buildings shown in the exhibit, 33 remain.

39. GIROD STREET CEMETERY   New Orleans, Louisiana, 1750—1957. Death was treated as a more familiar specter in the eighteenth and nineteenth centuries when the average life expectancy was far shorter. Enormous care was lavished on the design of cemeteries, tombstones, and other forms of funerary art. This view shows both the architecturally conceived mausoleum of the Lusitanos Benevolent Association, erected in 1853, and three of the characteristic New Orleans above-ground tombs. After more than two hundred years as sacred ground, this cemetery was deconsecrated, the bodies removed, and the site used for a post office garage and road widening.

40. CHRIST CHURCH, EPISCOPAL Hudson, Ohio, 1846–1929, Simeon Porter. Hudson is a delightful town with a number of well-preserved buildings, and a village green evocative of its' settlers New England roots. Simeon Porter, better known for his Federal style buildings, located his Carpenter's Gothic church on the green. When it was found to be in poor condition, the congregation replaced it with a Georgian Revival edifice.

41. LENOX REFERENCE LIBRARY Princeton Theological Seminary, Princeton, New Jersey, 1842–1955. This early exercise in the use of Gothic design on a college campus was razed to make way for a far larger, far less distinguished library building.

42. BROAD STREET METHODIST CHURCH   Richmond, Virginia, 1859–1968, Albert Lawrence West. A neat and compact Italianate design, distinguished by the semi-hexagonal arcaded portico and the octagonal tower. The site is now a parking lot.

43. CHURCH OF THE UNITY Springfield, Massachusetts, 1866/9 – c. 1960, Henry Hobson Richardson. This was Richardson's first important commission, and although it was certainly not one of his greatest works, it was of enormous interest as the fledgling effort of a major American architect. The general program was not original, but the powerful massing of forms, the use of medieval motifs stripped of archaeological references, and the rugged handling of the stone, were all prophetic. The congregation, many of whom had moved away from the area, sold the site to a commercial developer. The building has been destroyed, but the development never occurred. The site is now a weed patch.

46. BAPTIST FEMALE UNIVERSITY Raleigh, North Carolina, 1899–1967, G. A. Bauer. When the Baptist Female University moved to another site in 1925 (and eventually took a new name, Meredith College), the building was converted into an apartment-hotel called the Mansion Park. Presumably the tenants appreciated the elegance of the rounded towers, reminiscent, like many of New York's most elegant contemporary mansions, of a French chateau. Now a parking lot.

44. WHITE HALL University of Kentucky, Lexington, Kentucky, 1880/2–1969, H. P. McDonald. White Hall was sturdy and utilitarian rather than markedly beautiful. McDonald's design was a rather provincial version of the eclectic Italian Renaissance Revival popular a decade earlier in the urban centers. Nevertheless, it had associative values as one of the three original buildings of the University. Along with two other buildings, Carnegie Library and Patterson Hall, it was razed to provide a site for a high-rise building.

45. MUNSON-WILLIAMS-MEMORIAL, Utica, New York, Richard Morris Hunt, c. 1895–1957. The site of this substantial and unusual structure which originally housed the Oneida Historical Society, is now occupied by a gas station.

47. LAYTON ART GALLERY   Milwaukee, Wisconsin, 1885/7 — 1958, G. and W. Audsley. By going to a firm of London architects for their plans, the trustees of the Layton Art Gallery presented Milwaukee with a precocious example of the sort of academic Neo-Classicism that was to dominate the country's public buildings after its triumph at the Chicago World's Fair of 1893. After the Layton merged with the Milwaukee Art Institute to form the Milwaukee Art Center, the building was no longer needed. The site is now a parking lot.

48, 49. MADISON SQUARE PRESBYTERIAN CHURCH   New York,
N.Y., 1906—1920's, McKim, Mead and White. Stanford White
was shot to death on the rooftop of Madison Square Garden
by a deranged and jealous husband the year this jewel-box
of a church was completed. Like the architect, the neighborhood
was already doomed. Both commerce and fashion were moving
uptown, and within less than a quarter of a century the Garden
and the church would both be gone.

III. House & Home

From the day the *Mayflower* landed the idea that every family should occupy its own home, on its own plot of land, has been part of the American dream. It was a pursuit in which most of America's leading architects were happy to cooperate until they turned to making bigger plans during the building boom that followed World War II. Their output was copied eagerly by countless local builders and contractors. Since domestic buildings evidence changes in fashion rather more quickly than do more monumental structures, they form our best record of American tastes, foibles, values and styles in life and art.

The shifts in taste and fashion responsible for the delightful variety of American houses have also been major factors in the discard or abandonment of both small vernacular dwellings and grandiose mansions. Until an interest in antiques became stylish in the 1920's, the man with wealth or social ambition to build or maintain his own home would have been unlikely to consider anything but the latest style. Even after old houses, along with old furniture, old silver and old *objets d'art* graduated to the rank of status symbols, a certain degree of antiquity was requisite and might overwhelm considerations of quality. We are, for example, beginning to witness a strong resurgence of appreciation for Victorian houses. While they were out of style, however, great numbers were destroyed or "modernized" beyond recognition.

Fashion and economics often play a correlative role in determining the fate of private homes. When a neighborhood is no longer one that the "right people" consider desirable, its houses one by one become the possessions of those unable or unwilling to maintain them. Neglected and decaying, they eventually become prime candidates for destruction. An excessive rise in land values can also be a powerful incentive for calling in the bulldozer. The most vulnerable houses have been not only those in deteriorating neighborhoods, but also those in urban areas that prove convenient for the encroachment of commerce or those in once-rural communities in the process of transformation to suburbs.

America still retains an enormous number of older houses, many of them of relatively high quality. But numerically, the losses of domestic buildings far outstrip those in any other category. It is not an inexhaustible resource.

50. MACKAY HOUSE   Roslyn, Long Island, New York, 1902 – 1940's, McKim, Mead and White.

The vernacular urban buildings of the seventeenth and eighteenth centuries almost all disappeared by the end of the nineteenth century. Now those that remain in suburban and rural areas are being decimated. These buildings, with their survival of medieval designs and techniques from many parts of Europe, were the most concrete visual reminder of America's pluralistic roots. They provided the spice of variety as well as the appeal of antiquity on the American scene.

51. OLD FEATHER STORE   Boston, Massachusetts, 1680 – 1860. One of the last surviving seventeenth - century domestic buildings in downtown Boston, the Old Feather Store came down at approximately the same time as the Hancock House.
Both were sacrificed for the widening of North Street. Originally a frame structure, stuccoed over, the Old Feather Store reflected medieval English prototypes with its multiplicity of gables and the wide overhang of the second story.

52. THE TILE HOUSE   New Castle, Delaware, 1687 – 1884. A typical small Dutch urban dwelling, with its stepped gable turned to the street and the date of its construction indicated by iron numerals which also served as beam anchors, this was one of the last surviving houses of this type in the country. Allowed to disintegrate, it was finally demolished as a menace to safety.

53. CALEB CARR HOUSE   Jamestown, Rhode Island, c. 1680 – c. 1960. In this case, having a good photograph of this Rhode Island stone - ender may be almost as good as having what was left of the building. It had been, in a sense, already destroyed by extensive rebuilding before its actual destruction by fire.

54. MEAD FARM HOUSE   Rye, New York, c. 1690–1951. Being saved once isn't enough for some buildings. The photograph shows the Mead House in 1893, in a somewhat dilapidated condition. In 1902 it was reroofed, reshingled, and generally refurbished, in a manner which destroyed some of its interesting admixture of English and Dutch features, but did preserve the structure. Nevertheless, by the end of World War II it had once again been allowed to deteriorate; it had become so riddled by termites that restoration was impossible.

55. INNERWYCK (Brazier House) Flushing, Long Island, New York, c. 1680, c. 1780–1959. Innerwyck began as a small seventeenth-century Dutch dwelling. It was enlarged and altered to a typical two-and-a-half story Long Island farmhouse late in the eighteenth century, with much of the early interior detail preserved, however, in the earlier wing to the right. It was razed for a housing development.

56. INNERWYCK, detail, Dutch door.

57. MANSION FARM   vicinity of New Castle, Delaware, c. 1750 – 1961/2. A neat, trim farmhouse, with a facade reflecting
Georgian ideas of symmetry, but retaining in its verticality and pent roof elements of an earlier vernacular style. It was still in
excellent condition when it was destroyed during the construction of an industrial plant.

58. DRYSDALE GLEBE King and Queen County, Virginia, mid - 18th century — 1960's. Glebe houses, dedicated to the service of the parish and often used as rectories, are a distinctive Virginia form. Although they are small and may reflect, as this one did, the domestic designs of an earlier day, they are characterized by the fine workmanship usually reserved for manor houses and churches. Drysdale Glebe, destroyed by neglect, had magnificent Flemish checker brickwork.

EAPLICATION DES CHIFRES MARQUES CY DESSUS
1. maison de M. La pointe, de deux etages et un Balcon tout au tour
2. magazin qui est Fait 3 colomBier, 4 maison des negres, 5 la Forge 6 chap-
Projettee 7 autre magazin projetté. L sclerie a Bras M-Jardin o. Laiterie
P cuisine Q La cour, R·S· Vüe DE la mer T debarquement v La Rivierre

59. De la Pointe - Krebs House   Pascagoula, Mississippi, 1718 — mid - 19th c. In 1711, the Duchesse de Chaumont received a land grant from Louis XIV, in what was then French territory. To protect her interests she sent a fleet to the New World, headed by her brother, Admiral de la Pointe. This was the palisaded settlement they created in the wilderness. It included a two - story, verandahed mansion house, dove - cots, dairy, storehouse, slave quarter and numerous other outbuildings. Under the proprietorship of de La Pointe's son - in - law, Baron Frans von Krebs, it was operated as a feudal estate, producing cotton, indigo and rice. During the nineteenth century most of the buildings were allowed to disintegrate. Only one remains, the carpenter's shop, now known as "The Old Spanish Fort" and maintained as a museum.

60. Crane Homestead   Montclair, New Jersey, c. 1750 - c. 1900. Northeastern New Jersey once had great numbers of what are best classified as Dutch Colonial houses. The Crane House, with its ashlar walls, wooden gable, and slightly concave roof, was not a particularly distinguished architectural example, but it combined a good deal of charm with historic importance. It served as Washington's headquarters for three weeks in 1780. Despite efforts to save it, it was razed for a small housing development.

Thirty or forty years ago, a list of lost American buildings would have included dozens of great mansions of the eighteenth and early nineteenth centuries. For buildings of this sort, the rate of loss has slowed. There are few of them left and their kind has been appreciated for so long that they are almost immune from destruction. The smaller houses of the Georgian and Federal periods continue to go, this despite the fact that many of them possess a scale and accommodation for domestic comfort that make them eminently suitable for modern family living. After all, the "colonial center hall plan" is still a staple of contemporary mass-produced housing. What makes the difference between those houses that are still lived in, many of them lovingly restored and those that are lost? Usually, money. The houses in urban commercial centers or suburban locations near any expanding city are doomed, no matter how venerable or how beautiful they may be. The land is worth an astronomical sum for commercial development and few owners can afford to keep them.

61. EIGHTH AND ARCH STREETS   Philadelphia, Pennsylvania, mid-18th c. – c. 1875. Brick townhouses like these are restored and cherished today in Philadelphia's Society Hill area. But in other parts of that city, and in much of the country, the inevitability of destruction in the face of commercial development is still accepted, as it was by the proprietor of Wood's Trimming Store.

62. SPARHAWK HALL   Kittery, Maine, 1742 – 1965. Kittery proved to be too small a town to support two grandiose Georgian houses. The 1760 Lady Pepperrell Mansion still stands, restored and maintained by the Society for the Preservation of New England Antiquities. But the owners of Sparhawk could find no group willing to preserve their older house. In 1952 they sold the interior woodwork — the paneling, and the stair with its twisted balusters and pineapple finial on the newel — to a wealthy summer resident. In 1965 the remains of the house were sold to Strawbery Banke, a non-profit organization engaged in restoring a large area in the neighboring city of Portsmouth, New Hampshire. The bits and pieces of Sparhawk will be used in that restoration.

63. SPARHAWK HALL, detail, interior.

64. MENOKIN Richmond County, Virginia, 1769 – c. 1970. The Tayloes of Mount Airy built this house as a wedding present for their daughter on the occasion of her marriage to Francis Lightfoot Lee, later a signer of the Declaration of Independence. The house was unusually monumental, although its actual size was rather small. Treated by its present owners with hostile indifference, it is now simply a pile of stones.

65. PEIRCE HOUSE   Portsmouth, New Hampshire, c. 1785 – 1930's, (left); LEAVITT HOUSE   Portsmouth, New Hampshire, prior to 1761 – 1930's. These houses preceded their more grandiose neighbor in demolition by some 20 years. The sites are occupied by stores.

66. CUTTER HOUSE   Portsmouth, New Hampshire, c. 1750–1950's. A sophisticated Georgian mansion, distinguished by rusticated quoins and the use of triangular, segmental, and broken gables over the windows. An Italianate door had been substituted for the original, probably in the second half of the nineteenth century. The house to the left is the Leavitt House.

67. PEACE PARTY HOUSE   Pittsfield, Massachusetts, c. 1750 – 1957.   Later additions, including the portico, had not spoiled the handsome lines of this gambrel - roofed New England Georgian house. It was long a Pittsfield landmark, not only because of its appearance, but because in 1783 it had been the site of a great, never - forgotten party to celebrate the Treaty of Paris ending the Revolution.   It was demolished to provide a site for a new City Hall.   The City Hall was never built.   The site is now a parking lot.

68. JANVRIN - SHAPLEY HOUSE   Portsmouth, New Hampshire, c. 1750 – 1952. Had only ten years been added to the two centuries this house existed, it would undoubtedly still be preserved and probably restored. An automotive parts store was built on the site when the house was demolished. Only a decade later the store itself was demolished after the property was acquired by the Strawbery Banke restoration. The site is now a parking lot.

69. JANVRIN - SHAPLEY HOUSE detail, interior. Fortunately the beautiful interior woodwork, the most striking feature of the house, was removed and installed in a private dwelling.

70. PETER RHOADS HOUSE   Allentown, Pennsylvania, 1762 – 1968. The area's most important citizen of the Revolutionary era built his fine Georgian house the year Allentown was founded. It remained in its original state until early in the twentieth century when it was converted to commercial use. It had been defaced beyond recognition by the time it was demolished to provide space for a parking lot.

71. SPENCE HOUSE   Portsmouth, New Hampshire, c. 1750 – 1930's. The Spence House and the barn - like structure behind it were razed; a gas station was built on the site. Now the gas station is no longer in use. The pumps have been removed and the windows boarded up. Only the near half of the double house to the left of the barn is still standing, in use as an office. A modern two - story commercial building, occupies the site of the far half. The site of the large house to the left is now a parking lot.

72. NATHANIEL WALKER HOUSE   Sturbridge, Massachusetts, c. 1775 – c. 1960. A pleasant New England one-and-a-half story gambrel - roofed country house, with unpretentious, but well - proportioned paneling. It was torn down during development of a state recreation area.

73. NATHANIEL WALKER HOUSE, detail, interior.

74. JOHN DICKINSON HOUSE   Wilmington, Delaware, c. 1785 – 1926. A substantial and elegant townhouse, built in two stages. Dickinson was a signer of both the Declaration of Independence and the Constitution. Another building has been erected on the site.

75. Conrad House   Winchester, Virginia, late 18th c. — 1970. A fine example of a late Georgian house with Federal detailing. The site is now a parking lot.

76. HAMPTON PLACE Elizabeth, New Jersey, 1783 - 1926. The retirement home of General Winfield Scott, hero of the War of 1812 and the Mexican War, was a generous Federal mansion, added to a smaller, earlier house. It was razed to provide a site for a gasoline station.

77. HOUSTON - SCREVEN HOUSE Savannah, Georgia, 1784 — 1920. An unusual and sophisticated hallway, with a groin vaulted, plaster ceiling and beautifully proportioned woodwork. Demolished.

78. HAMILTON-HOFFMAN HOUSE   Philadelphia, Pennsylvania, 1791 / 1800 – 1959. This house had beautifully detailed Federal interiors, the inner hall doorway being especially fine. It was demolished by the city to provide a site for a school.

79. SWANWYCK vicinity of New Castle, Delaware, 1813/19 — c.1950. Built by Peter Bauduy for his daughter and son - in - law, this small and delicately - scaled house was one of the few American buildings designed in the style of the English Regency. It has been altered beyond recognition.

80. WILLIAM WATSON HOUSE · Providence, Rhode Island, 1818–1955, John Holden Greene. This small, compact, but finely detailed Federal house was razed to make way for the expansion of Brown University. The Shepard House, a fine, advanced Greek Revival house by Russell Warren, was demolished at the same time and for the same purpose.

81. BARNWELL HOUSE   Beaufort, South Carolina, c. 1800 – 1883. Sophisticated builders in the Federal period delighted in the interplay of round and elliptical forms with simple rectangular shapes. The curving exterior staircase leading to the semi-circular portico of this double house was exceptionally fine. Converted to use as a courthouse, the building eventually burned.

82. HILDRETH HOUSE Marietta, Ohio, c.1824 – early 1960's, attributed to Col. Joseph Barker. Marietta, the first organized American settlement of the old Northwest Territory, possessed a number of exceptionally fine early nineteenth - century structures. This one became the property of the county, which no longer wished to maintain it.

83. PROSPECT HILL   Airlie, Halifax County, North Carolina,
1825 / 8 – post World War II, attributed to Burgess of Virginia.
A house deriving great distinction from the elegance and
attenuation of the detail. The use of Palladian windows
throughout the facade is unusual and imaginative.

84. PROSPECT HILL, rear elevation. The loggia, with its
unusually attenuated columns, was a feature unique to this
and a few other houses in the vicinity.

85. WILLIAM DE WOLFE HOUSE (also known as Middleton House)   Bristol, Rhode Island, 1808 – c. 1950, Russell Warren. A very fine Federal house by Rhode Island's most famous early nineteenth - century architect. It had a superb circular staircase. Demolished.

86. RANDALL MANSION   Cortland, New York, 1828 – 1943.   Built by a wealthy merchant, this was the most elaborate house ever constructed in Cortland.   The pilastered facade and a spiral staircase were its most impressive features.   A proposal that the city purchase and restore the mansion failed in a 1936 referendum.   The plot was developed for commercial use.

87. MONTEBELLO Baltimore, Maryland, 1799–1909. This was an unusual and graceful house. A portico featuring concave curves led to a one-story rectangular wing. This was backed by a two-story wing with semicircular ends. The interplay of shapes continued within; the dining room was oval, and the drawing room terminated in one of the semicircular bays. The whole was handled with great delicacy and nicety of proportion.

88. HARPER HOUSE   Baltimore, Maryland, c. 1820 – 1931, attributed to Benjamin Henry Latrobe. The house is generally attributed to Latrobe on the basis of the monumental simplicity of the restrained classic facade and his close friendship with its original owner, Robert Goodloe Harper. It was demolished for a building site by the Enoch Pratt Free Library.

89. Joseph Bowers House   Northampton, Massachusetts, 1825/6 — 1916, Ithiel Town. With its magnificent Ionic colonnade, this was one of the great monuments of the domestic Greek Revival. The wide dissemination of this view, drawn by Town's partner, Alexander Jackson Davis, may have helped to popularize the format of a central temple flanked by lower wings.

90. WITHERSPOON HOUSE   Rochester, N.Y. c. 1832–1968. A simple, vernacular house, gaining distinction from its free and imaginative use of Greek forms, exemplified by the deep raking cornice, unexpectedly adorned with mutules. In the path of a projected highway, it was demolished.

91. CHARLES WHITE HOUSE   Norwich, Connecticut, 1832 – c. 1960. Norwich had a number of restrained and dignified Greek Revival houses. This one was removed to provide a site for a new church.

92. DEAN RICHMOND HOUSE Batavia, New York, 1838-1970. The Erie Canal, completed in 1825, brought enormous prosperity to northwestern New York, just at the time that the Greek Revival was at its height. As a result, the area was eventually studded with substantial houses with colonnaded porticos and fashionable Greek trim. The Richmond house, enlarged and classicized in 1853 for one of the organizers of the New York Central Railroad, was the last large house of the period in Batavia preserved in any reasonable semblance of its appearance in its heyday.

93. DEAN RICHMOND HOUSE, demolition. The house was destroyed by the town's Board of Education after a three-year fight with the local Landmark Society. The land is now a parking lot.

94. HOMEWOOD   vicinity of Natchez, Mississippi, 1855 – 1940.
One of the grandiose late Greek Revival houses of the South,
with extravagantly lavish trim and particularly beautiful
ironwork. Burned.

95. ALFRED KELLEY HOUSE   Columbus, Ohio, 1837–1961. The home of Alfred Kelley, legislator, financier and benefactor of the state of Ohio, was one of the most elaborate examples of the Greek Revival in the Midwest. It was dismantled, stone by stone, to provide a site for a new hotel. The stones have been piled on the state fairgrounds awaiting possible reassembly on a new site.

96. MOUNT AIRY   Danville, Ky., mid-19th c. — after 1940. Like many Greek Revival buildings built in rather remote areas, this one exhibited crisp, clean details and elegant proportions, although in rather simpler form than would have been found in the great urban centers.

97. MOFFATT-HEUSTIS HOUSE   Terre Haute, Indiana, 1852 – 1906. The "four-column" house with side wings was common wherever the Greek Revival style was executed. It is especially associated, however, with western New York, moving from there to Ohio, Michigan, Indiana and Illinois. Its persistent popularity is indicated by the late date of this building. The site became the Training School of the Indiana State Teachers College.

98. UNCLE SAM Convent, Louisiana, 1849 – 1940, view from south *garçonniere* (overseer's house) towards mansion. W. Darrell Overdyke in *Louisiana Plantation Homes* described this as "The most extensive, the best executed and perhaps the most beautiful ante-bellum plantation complex in Louisiana." Certainly it was one of the most elaborately Greek; of its forty buildings, five, the mansion, the two flanking *garçonnieres*, office and kitchen all boasted full colonnades. Despite last minute efforts by the National Park Service to save it, it was destroyed when encroachment by the Mississippi forced the rebuilding of the levee.

99. BELLE GROVE near White Castle, Louisiana, 1857 – 1952, attributed to Henry Howard. Perhaps the epitome of the great Southern mansion was Belle Grove. Executed in brick, plastered over and painted pink, it was a far cry from the restrained simplicity of the forms of the early Greek Revival. Rather, this was a Victorian house, lavish in scale and irregular in outline. The detail, however, was still mainly Greek, with some Italianate touches. The elaborate Corinthian columns were carved from blocks of cypress six feet high. All the decor was equally extravagant. Even the doorknobs were silver. Abandoned in 1914, nibbled at by the floodwaters of the Mississippi, the house disintegrated into ruin until it was finally destroyed by fire.

While the Greek Revival was still the preferred style for most domestic building in the 1830's, progressive architects began to offer their clients a choice of other modes loosely based on past periods. These were disseminated widely in books and magazine articles, the most prolific and popular exponent of the new styles being Andrew Jackson Downing. Prospective home-builders were offered an almost bewildering array. There were Swiss chalets; Romanesque, Norman and Italianate villas; Moorish, Oriental and Byzantine houses; and everything in Gothic from bracketed cottages to battlemented castles. From this visual smorgasbord, the public adopted the Gothic and Italianate forms with the most enthusiasm. Whatever their skins, these houses offered a freedom of plan not possible within the rigid symmetry of the preceding classical styles. They were also considered particularly suitable to an emerging and quintessentially American type — the suburban house.

100. GLEN ELLEN near Towson, Maryland, 1832 – 1929, Alexander Jackson Davis. Although Latrobe had designed a house called Sedgeley near Philadelphia utilizing Gothic detail as early as 1799, Glen Ellen is generally considered the first full-blown house of the Gothic Revival in America. Davis, who is said to have modeled this building on Sir Walter Scott's "Abbotsford," became the country's foremost designer of Gothic Revival houses. This one was destroyed by the city of Baltimore and the site used for a reservoir.

101. RIVERSIDE Burlington, New Jersey, 1837 – 1961, John Notman. The first American villa in the Italianate style was built for Bishop George Washington Doane by Notman, who had arrived in Philadelphia from Scotland in 1832. Presumably he was therefore familiar with the Italianate designs Charles Barry already was executing in England in the late 1820's. Despite its Italianate tower and round-arched doorway, Riverside had Gothic interiors. Demolished.

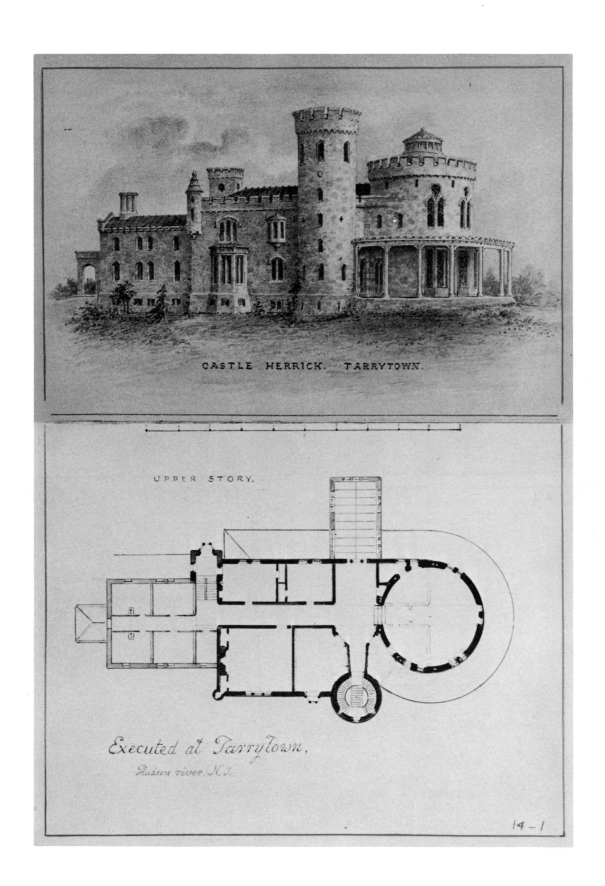

CASTLE HERRICK. TARRYTOWN.

UPPER STORY.

Executed at Tarrytown,
Hudson river, N.Y.

14-1

102. HERRICK'S CASTLE (also known as Ericstan)   Tarrytown, New York, c. 1855–1944, A. J. Davis.
Perched on a hill overlooking the Hudson River, Herrick's Castle, turreted and castellated, was a most
impressive pile. Converted to use as a girl's school, it was demolished when the tract was sold for a
housing development.

103. SEDGWICK HOUSE   Syracuse, New York, 1845 / ff. – 1962, A. J. Davis. The front section
of this house was the archetype of the bracketed Gothic cottage. The rear portions, added later,
were more castle - like, but in keeping with the earlier work. The Sedgwick House stood on
James Street, one of Syracuse's most elegant avenues, lined with distinguished nineteenth -
century houses. Among them was a fine Greek Revival House, the Leavenworth House, erected
in 1838. Like the Sedgwick House, they have all been demolished.

104. MUDGE HOUSE   Lynn, near Swampscott, Massachusetts, 1842 – late 1950's, Isaiah Rogers.
A Gothic cottage of great charm, designed by an architect best known for his Greek Revival
hotels and commercial buildings. The diaper-patterned masonry was of particular interest.

105. BUCKINGHAM - CHAPPELEAR HOUSE   Zanesville, Ohio, c.1855 – 1948. Like the Greek Revival, the Gothic Revival spread westward from the Atlantic seaboard. This handsome batten - and - board example had richly ornamented interiors, and Bohemian glass insets in the front door and at the tops of the first floor windows. The site is now a used car lot.

106. JEWETT - STETSON HOUSE   Bangor, Maine, 1851 – 1969, attributed to Benjamin S. Deane. This was basically a four - square house, not highly advanced in terms of plan or basic shape. Its glory was its plethora of Italianate ornament. Even the fenceposts echoed the forms of the brackets adorning the eaves and porticos. Demolished.

107. YATES CASTLE Syracuse, New York, 1852/3 — early 1950's, James Renwick, Jr. One of the country's most talented architects of the mid-nineteenth century, best known for the Smithsonian Institution and New York's St. Patrick's Cathedral, designed one of his rare private residences for C. T. Longstreet. Longstreet, a clothier, had made a fortune shipping ready-made suits to California during the Gold Rush. His castle eventually became the property of Syracuse University. It was destroyed to provide a site for a medical school.

108. DUNLEATH Greensboro, North Carolina, 1856 – 1968. A Swiss chalet with Italianate features, thought to have been based on one of the many drawings published by Samuel Sloan. It was used as general headquarters during the Union Army's occupation. The house was demolished to make way for an apartment complex which has never been built.

109. STEVENS CASTLE, interior, stairhall.

110. STEVENS CASTLE   Hoboken, New Jersey, 1854 – 1959. It has never been established who designed the Stevens family mansion, although it has been variously attributed to John Notman, Samuel Sloan, and A. J. Davis. Built with the proceeds of one of the first great railroad fortunes, it crowned a bluff with a magnificent view of New York Harbor. Given by the Stevens family to Stevens Institute of Technology, it was last used as an alumni center. Although a majority of the school's alumni were in favor of saving it, it was demolished. The executive secretary of the alumni association, describing it as a "monstrosity," said, "It occupies a million dollar site that could better be used for a greater landmark." His greater landmark? A rather routine, 12 - story steel and glass box.

111. WYMAN VILLA Baltimore, Maryland, 1853–1955, attributed to Richard Upjohn. The attribution seems likely since this was an almost exact replica of Upjohn's villa for Edward King (now being restored in Newport, Rhode Island), as shown in Design XXVIII in Downing's *The Architecture of Country Houses*. Willed to Johns Hopkins University, the house was allowed to disintegrate. It was razed for a parking lot even though a committee was attempting to raise funds to preserve and restore it.

112. Harral-Wheeler House   Bridgeport, Connecticut, 1846–1958, A. J. Davis.   The fate of this house, a mature masterpiece by Davis, is one of the classic tragedies of building loss. Carefully preserved by its last owner, Archer C. Wheeler, with many of its original furnishings intact, the house was bequeathed to the city. Mr. Wheeler specified that the building be devoted to educational and park uses and provided a fund for its upkeep.   Nevertheless, the city filed suit to tear the house down in order to use the site for a new city hall and civic center. Outraged citizens protested and picketed.   When election time came they elected a mayor who ran on a platform that included a promise to preserve the house if money could be raised for necessary repairs. Before the fund-raising project could get well under way, the house was demolished. Some of the interiors have been installed in the Smithsonian.

The second half of the nineteenth century and the early years of the twentieth were a period of ferment and vitality in American architecture. The established styles persisted, but were elaborated, and motifs from various sources were often freely combined in one building. In the decades following the Civil War, "mansard madness" swept the country. The curving roofs of the French Second Empire were used to cap houses whose detailing might be Greek, Italianate, Gothic, or an eclectic mixture. The late '70's brought, among the more advanced architects and clients, a return to simpler forms and a stress on the inherent, natural qualities of materials. Some free and highly inventive work was done in the '80's and '90's, only to be superseded in popularity by a new wave of revival styles, handled in a drier and more archaeological manner than the revivals of the earlier part of the century.

114. ROUND HOUSE Middletown, Rhode Island, c. 1865–c. 1955, Christopher Southwick. Whether this was a variant on Fowler's scheme or a unique creation of its shipwright builder, the Middletown house was an architectural curiosity. It had an hour-glass hall, three oval-shaped rooms, and some odd nooks and crannies on each floor. Burned.

113. WILLIAM S. CHARNLEY HOUSE New Haven, Connecticut, 1853 – 1913, Henry Austin. In 1847 one Orson Squire Fowler published a book called *A Home for All, or the Gravel Wall and Octagon Mode of Building, New Cheap, Convenient, Superior, and Adapted to Rich and Poor*. Enough people got the message so that hundreds of octagon houses were built between the Atlantic and the Mississippi, even if not all of them had gravel walls. The Charnley House was a fine example of the genre by a first - rate architect.

115. HENRY W. OLIVER HOUSE   Pittsburgh, Pennsylvania, 1871–1967. A suitably substantial Italianate mansion for a Pittsburgh magnate, with pleasant proportions, this was razed as part of a plan for a new community college campus.

116. WEDNESDAY CLUB   Danville, Virginia, 1884 – 1969. A simple, but well - proportioned late Italianate house with a delicate cast iron porch, this was torn down to make way for erection of a contemporary clubhouse.

117. PERKINS – CLARK HOUSE   Hartford, Connecticut, c. 1855 - 1958. A dignified and restrained example of the "swell front" urban mansion. On Mrs. Clark's death in 1938, the house was offered to the Hartford Public Library, it having been her wish that "the property might serve some publicly beneficial use." The Library has moved from the area; the house was sold to the Travelers Insurance Company which demolished it for an addition to its offices.

118. THOMPSON HOUSE   Rochester, New York, 1877–1968. George H. Thompson, a contractor, built this house for himself, using the finest materials and the best of skilled craftsmanship, plus fashionable Eastlake detailing on the window and door surrounds. It stood on Rochester's street of great mansions, East Avenue, until demolished by an owner who did not wish to make the repairs necessary to bring it into conformity with the city's building code.

119. BENJAMIN WADE HOUSE   Jefferson, Ohio, c. 1865–1969. Wade, a Radical Republican, was Ohio's most prominent spokesman in the Civil War era. As President *pro tem* of the Senate, he would have succeeded to the Presidency had the impeachment proceedings against Andrew Johnson been upheld.

120. HARRIES HOUSE Dayton, Ohio, 1867 – 1954. Set in the middle of an 162 - acre estate, the house was built for a wealthy entrepreneur and manufacturer. After the death of his las t surviving daughter in 1952, the building was literally destroyed by vandals. When arsonists set it on fire, the trustees of the estate had the remains of the house razed.

121. BEECHWOOD (Jedidiah Wilcox House)   Meriden, Connecticut, 1868 / 70 – 1970. A fortune based on hoopskirts and carpetbags paid for one of Connecticut's most elaborate mid - Victorian mansions, supposedly to the tune of $200,000 for house, grounds and furnishings. Three of the mansion's forty rooms — the hall, parlor, and sitting room — have been removed to the Metropolitan Museum of Art, where they will be installed, along with some of their original furnishings, in the American Wing.

124. ALFRED UIHLEIN HOUSE Milwaukee, Wisconsin, c. 1887–1970, attributed to Henry C. Koch. Built for an executive of the Schlitz Brewing Company, this was one of a series of imposing houses for members of the same family in an affluent neighborhood that came to be known as "Uihlein Hill." Donated to the Archdiocese of Milwaukee, the house survived in remarkably good condition until it was razed in the course of an urban renewal project. The neighborhood has been rezoned for light industry.

122, 123. PRESIDENT GRANT'S COTTAGE Long Branch, New Jersey, 1866–1963. An engagingly flimsy-looking seaside Tudor cottage, built when Long Branch was a fashionable resort. It had been stripped of its vaguely Gothic porches and the roofline had been much changed long before its final demolition.

125. CYRUS McCORMICK HOUSE   Richfield Springs, New York, 1882 – c. 1958, McKim, Mead and White. The building designed as a summer home for the millionaire inventor of the reaper was one of the most exciting Shingle Style houses. The bold interplay of triangular and horizontal shapes, penetrated by the voids of porches, was emphasized rather than disguised by a frill of lighthearted ornament. The house has been allowed to fall into ruin.

126. CYRUS McCORMICK HOUSE, Stable. The rich textural effect possible in the use of natural wood shingles was rarely displayed better than in this outbuilding. The impact is heightened by the contrast with the inset mosaic panels. The stable still stands, but if its present neglect continues, it will suffer the same fate as the house.

127. Low House Bristol, Rhode Island, 1887–1960's, McKim, Mead and White. Generally acknowledged as one of the masterpieces of the Shingle Style, with its design reduced to a single bold, sweeping triangle. It was torn down by private owners who bought the property for the ocean view and erected a nondescript house on the site.

128. BARNEY MANSION   Dayton, Ohio, 1891 – 1969, P. R. Gilbert. This was one of many substantial houses built in the late 1880's and the 90's based on the Romanesque forms popularized by Henry Hobson Richardson. Most of them were built in urban neighborhoods. As the wealthier city residents flee to the suburbs, these buildings tend to be converted to commercial use. This one was first a Knights of Columbus hall and then a funeral home, before being purchased by a real estate group that is holding the land for development. To reduce taxes, they razed the building and are using the site for a parking lot.

129. FLOOD HOUSE   Appomattox Court House, Virginia, 1911 – 1970. From the last decade of the nineteenth century to the present, the revival of America's own favored styles of the past has been a popular motif, especially for the homes of the well - to - do. Neo - Colonial and Neo - Classical houses abound in America's old and new suburbs. As neighborhoods change, many of these too will be lost, as this one was, to commercial development.

130. LONGWOOD   Cleveland Heights, Ohio, c. 1920 – 1960, Charles Schweinfurth. This great English Tudor Revival estate house was one of many (several of which have been destroyed) built by Schweinfurth for the wealthy burghers of the Cleveland area. Although there was much local protest, the site was purchased for a shopping center, and the house and most of the grounds were destroyed.

131. TIFFANY HOUSE   Oyster Bay, Long Island, New York, 1904 – 1957, Louis Comfort Tiffany. The house itself was not much — a great, rambling, vaguely Moorish pile dominated by a clock tower. But the site was superb and Tiffany lavished all his genius on the decor. By the time he was through, he was reputed to have spent $13 million on the place. Burned.

132, 133. TIFFANY HOUSE, details, interior. Marble, glass, mosaics, gilded bronze, all were used with a free, but subtle hand.

134. Clarence H. Mackay House Roslyn, Long Island, New York, 1902–1940's, McKim, Mead and White. Like many of the palatial suburban estates of the early twentieth century, the Mackays' chateau was abandoned when maintenance became too expensive during the Depression. The house finally burned, and the estate is now a housing development.

IV. Commerce & Industry

"In democracies," Alexis de Tocqueville noted, "nothing is greater or more brilliant than commerce . . . all energetic passions are directed towards it." It is thus both natural and fitting that the first building form in which American architects gained world dominance should be the tall office building. The inventions and technological innovations that made the tall building possible — structural iron and steel, fireproof materials, the power - driven elevator — origina - ted both here and abroad. But they were developed in America with an intensity and energy unrivalled elsewhere. Now the same restless search that impelled this development has also led to the replacement of once - noteworthy buildings by newer and larger structures.

Often, however, the real villain is not building obsolescence but the somewhat quirky nature of the economic factors, tax policies and government regulations concerning real estate. The older build - ing on the single block assembled long ago — Ernest Flagg's Singer Building in New York City is an example — goes, while around it may remain blocks devoted to nondescript smaller buildings, vacant lots and parking garages. The process certainly doesn't do much for the townscape and the net gain in office space is not as great as it might be. But buying the assembled block is cheaper and less time - consuming for the developer than dealing with the individual owners of the several undeveloped parcels. And then, because of building laws that allow "accelerated depreciation" to encourage new building, it may well be more profitable to tear down the old skyscraper and put a new one.

Of course, obsolescence and changes in business practices do play their part. Not every grist mill or textile plant can become a museum. Commercial buildings were, after all, designed for functional purposes. We most admire those in which the aesthetic appeal is derived from acceptance of functional needs and the directness with which those needs were met. Some form of genuine continued function must be found for these buildings if they are to be saved.

136. ERIE COUNTY SAVINGS BANK   Buffalo, New York, 1890/3 – 1968, George B. Post. A peculiar combination of backward and progressive architecture, with steel frame interior construction and masonry bearing walls.

Colonial and post-Revolutionary America was basically a society of farmers and merchant-traders. Its industrial needs were few. Mills were needed to grind grain, to saw wood, to full cloth. The buildings that encompassed the necessary machinery were simple and strictly functional. They had few architectural pretensions, but at their best they often displayed the craft of fine building.

137. NEWMAN MILL   Stamford, Connecticut, 1726 – 1969. If the loss of the Harral-Wheeler House was a tragedy, the destruction of the Newman Mill was, literally, a crime. Built as a grist mill, it had operated continuously until 1918, after which the building stood empty but with machinery from three periods of operation intact. The mill was located on seven and one-half acres which had been donated to the city of Stamford as a park. Almost all the funds necessary for its restoration as a working grist mill had been raised; drawings and specifications were complete. It was burned by arsonists.

138. LE VAN MILL   Kutztown, Pennsylvania, 1732 – c. 1960.   Aside from its interest as an early industrial structure, the mill built by Jacob Le Van, a Huguenot, had other historical associations.   Count Zinzendorf, a missionary to the Moravians, is said to have preached from its balcony in 1742.   The mill has collapsed into ruin.

139. IRVINE MILL   Irvinesburg (now Russell), Pennsylvania, 1834 – 1962. A simple rectangular building, but obviously erected by a master mason. Note in particular the handling of the stones of the corner quoins. After being allowed to deteriorate for years, the building was demolished, and the stones used elsewhere.

140. HORNER'S ORIGINAL MILL   Eaton Rapids, Michigan, 1846 – 1966. Built as a grist mill, this was converted to the manufacture of woolens. It was extensively used by the Horners in their advertisements in the 1880's. Along with the canal that once provided it with power, it was a valuable reminder of the early days of Michigan industry.

141. KING'S SMITHY   St. Augustine, Florida, 1793 – 1898. This was the dwelling for the Spanish government's master blacksmith, erected to replace a still earlier dwelling and forge on the same site. Originally the Smithy was a two-story building. The masonry lower story contained the forge room and dwelling area; the upper story, perhaps a storeroom, was of wood. All but the dwelling room deteriorated into ruin between 1855 and 1880. This last remaining portion of the building was razed.

For a great many people in still-agrarian nineteenth-century America, business meant farming. Barns and other outbuildings dominated rural scenery. Some of these — the sloping Dutch barns of northern New Jersey and parts of New York, the stone and timber structures decorated with hex signs of the Pennsylvania Dutch — reflected their builders' antecedents. Others had more architectural pretensions; still others were original design solutions expressive of the structure's functional character.

142. BARN, HAYFIELD Fairfax County, Virginia, c. 1887–1967. The Hayfield Farm once belonged to George Washington, and later to members of his family. Its 16-sided barn, 100 feet in diameter and 100 feet high, is said to have been patterned after one belonging to the General. When the property was purchased for a subdivision, the barn was extensively used in the development's advertising. It was subsequently vandalized and burned.

143. CARRIAGE HOUSE AND STABLES Ravensworth, Fairfax County, Virginia, c. 1800 – 1960. These were the remaining buildings of a plantation built by the grandfather of Mrs. Robert E. Lee. It was to Ravensworth that Mrs. Lee removed when Arlington House was occupied by the Federal government during the Civil War. The mansion house was burned by arsonists in 1926. The Jeffersonian Classic carriage house was destroyed for development of a subdivision.

Early commercial buildings followed the domestic styles of their day and region. Offices and banks were often scarcely differentiated, even in plan, from the houses of the bankers and merchants who owned them. This remained the case, especially in smaller cities and towns, until well into the nineteenth century. In the larger urban centers, where more sophisticated architects might be commissioned to design such structures, polished schemes for the internal arrangements of commercial buildings were more frequent. Even when the functional nature of the building was expressed on the exterior, however, it was clothed in one of the fashionable revival styles of the romantic era.

144. OLD SPANISH MARKET   Natchez, Mississippi, late 18th c. – 1925. There are echoes of the monumental late Renaissance style brought to the Mississippi during the period of Spanish rule in the pillared and pilastered facade of the Market House. It was demolished to provide a site for a new city hall.

145. OLD LAWYERS' ROW   Natchez, Mississippi, c. 1787 – c. 1930. This one - story row, with its repeated rhythm of window, door and chimney, might almost be in one of the Spanish settlements of the southwest. The materials, however, were different — stuccoed brick rather than adobe. This is one of those buildings whose absence could not be borne. After it was demolished to provide space for a parking lot, it was eventually rebuilt on the same site, using old materials.

146. BANK OF PENNSYLVANIA   Philadelphia, Pennsylvania, 1798/1801 – c. 1870, Benjamin Henry Latrobe. Scholars generally credit this as the first Greek Revival building in America. Its main feature was a circular domed banking room, lighted by large arched windows in the sides of the building and the crowning octagonal cupola. When it was demolished at least some of the Ionic columns were used elsewhere. One has been identified serving as the pedestal of an urn in the Civil War monument at Adrian, Michigan.

East Front on Second Street.   *B Henry Latrobe del'd de f...*
1800

147. PLANTERS AND MECHANICS BANK   Charleston, South Carolina, c. 1830 – 1957. This was one of the more delightful examples of small Greek Revival buildings in which the detail was handled freely and imaginatively. For instance, griffons were used as a decorative element in the cornice rather than more traditional Greek motifs. It was demolished for a parking lot. Fortunately, the fascinating little Moorish structure at the right, the old Farmers and Exchange Bank, built in the late 1850's, did not suffer the same fate. It has since been restored as Senator Ernest F. Hollings local office.

148. STATE BANK OF GEORGIA   Savannah, Georgia, 1816 – 1906, William Jay. Jay's
domestically - scaled brick building utilized the delicate classicism of the English Regency,
rather than the more robust classic forms of the American Greek Revival. That he could
also design in the more monumental style was evidenced in his branch Bank of the
United States, also in Savannah, built in 1819 and demolished in 1924.

149, 150. EASTERN BANK   Bangor, Maine, 1834 – 1970. The Eastern Bank, with its crested tower and elaborate grillwork, made an impressive terminus to the simpler Federal and Greek Revival stores and warehouses of Bangor's Mercantile Row. The large building in the background of the lithograph from the cover of the "Bangor March" is the Bangor House, the last of Isaiah Rogers' Greek Revival hotels still in operation.

NORTH FRONT OF MERCANTILE ROW WITH A N.E. DISTANT FRONT OF THE BANGOR HOUSE

BANGOR MARCH,

151. THE BLEACHERY   Waltham, Massachusetts, c. 1820–1967. This was the second bleachery in the country, and one of the earliest of the water-powered textile mills. Like many early New England mills, its main building was crowned by a Georgian belfry challenging in height the spire or belfry of the town church. The site is now occupied by a shopping center.

The earliest planned industrial communities in America were the mill towns of the New England textile industry. Their buildings tended to be conservative. The planning was generally left in the hands of engineers and mill superintendents, although Asher Benjamin served for three years as agent of the Nashua Manufacturing Company, and his pupil, Samuel Shepherd designed some of the early buildings of the Amoskeag Manufacturing Company of Manchester, New Hampshire. The general conservatism of the design of these mill complexes may be responsible for the often pleasing result. The repeated use of the same material — in most instances brick — and the reiteration of simple design units based on the rather classical proportions of the Federal style gave unity and overall coherence even to complexes that were laid out over a long period of time.

THE BLEACHERY AT WALTHAM, MASSACHUSETTS.

152. The New Block, Merrimack Corporation   Lowell, Massachusetts, c. 1845 – 1966. Lowell was laid out as a utopian mill town, and its earlier buildings reflected the conservative dignity of metropolitan Boston, with neat and commodious structures for the accommodation of the workers. Those of the New Block were, in fact, less human in scale than the earlier Brick Block of 1825, and succeeding construction diminished the amenities of the complex. Both this and the Brick Block were demolished as part of an urban renewal project.

153. Merrimack Canal and Cotton Mill   Lowell, Massachusetts, 1863 – c. 1935. In visual terms, the vista at Lowell was perhaps most impressive when it was terminated by the picturesque tower of the cotton mill.

154. WAREHOUSE, DETROIT AND CLEVELAND NAVIGATION COMPANY   Detroit, Michigan, 1854 – c. 1955. Even though the designs of industrial buildings might be conservative, their builders did not hesitate to take advantage of improvements in technology. These handsomely detailed cast iron sills and lintels added grace, at no additional expense, to an otherwise straightforward building.

155. KEESEVILLE New York, c. 1850. The waters of the AuSable River provided the power for industrial development in Keese-ville as early as 1800. By mid-century the riverbanks were lined with sandstone factories, and the town endowed with substantial houses and a Gothic church. Keeseville has been luckier than some of the New England towns. The industries have changed, but most of the mills are still operating. Still fire and flood have taken their toll. The mill just above the bridge is gone and those at the left have been replaced by more modern structures, altering the unity of scale and design the town once possessed.

156. AMOSKEAG MANUFACTURING COMPANY Manchester, New Hampshire, 1838–late 1960's. A giant
among New England mill complexes. Amoskeag grew
over a period of 75 years. Its many buildings, ranging
from decorous Federal rows to High Victorian tower -
studded blocks, were unified by material and the regular
rhythms of fenestration. Now over a period of years the
integrity of the design is being destroyed as buildings
are demolished to provide space for roads and parking.

Many designers of commercial buildings in the second half of the nineteenth century, and well into the twentieth, continued to approach such commissions in the same way their predecessors had. Men like George B. Post and Cass Gilbert still bent currently fashionable styles to new uses, even when they incorporated sophisticated technological advances into their buildings. Meanwhile, more progressive architects were seeking fresh design solutions from the ground up. The interplay between the two approaches created one of the most exciting eras in American architecture.

159. THE JAYNE BUILDING   Philadelphia, Pennsylvania, 1849 / 51 – 1957, William J. Johnston.   A pioneering prototype of the skyscraper and created for a purveyor of patent medicines, the Jayne Building established the visual analogy to a column, the tripartite division of the facade into base, shaft and capital, that would be followed in tall buildings for decades to come. It was demolished under a plan for renewal of the area adjacent to Independence National Historical Park.

157. LAING STORES   New York, New York, 1848 – 1971, James Bogardus.   Bogardus patented and popularized a building system using prefabricated iron elements. Although iron as a structural material was not so quickly accepted, and, in fact, was not used by him in this particular building, iron fronts became enormously popular in all parts of the country. The warehouse for Edward Laing was the last of Bogardus' buildings left in New York City. Although elements of the facade have been stored for possible reassembly on another site, much of the original exterior cast iron ornament and all of the building's interior have been lost.

158. WARREN BUILDING   Troy, New York, 1870 – 1969.   Iron fronts could be assembled quickly and with relatively little skill, giving a semblance of artistic design to the simplest of buildings. Their pre-cast ornament often displayed a sophistication and quality of craftsmanship that local carvers would have been hard put to duplicate in stone or wood. Many were shipped from such great centers of the industry as Philadelphia and New York to California during the Gold Rush. It is not known whether this nicely proportioned example of the genre was cast in Troy or sent to that city from New York. Vacated in the course of an urban renewal project, it had attracted the attention of a buyer willing to restore it when it was burned by arsonists.

160. NATIONAL EXCHANGE BANK Hartford, Connecticut, 1835/rebuilt 1869 – 1917. The rebuilding maintained the domestic scale of what had evidently been a Greek Revival building, substituting for Greek detail the then more fashionable and rather ornate motifs of the Renaissance Revival. The building was replaced by a Chinese restaurant.

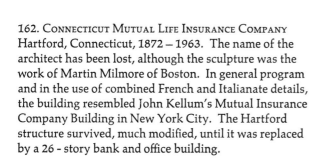

161. Aetna Insurance Company Hartford, Connecticut, 1867 – 1903. A restrained and handsome brownstone building, not unlike contemporary Renaissance Revival mansions. Its replacement was a massive example of Beaux - Arts Classicism.

162. Connecticut Mutual Life Insurance Company Hartford, Connecticut, 1872 – 1963. The name of the architect has been lost, although the sculpture was the work of Martin Milmore of Boston. In general program and in the use of combined French and Italianate details, the building resembled John Kellum's Mutual Insurance Company Building in New York City. The Hartford structure survived, much modified, until it was replaced by a 26 - story bank and office building.

163. PROVIDENT LIFE AND TRUST COMPANY   Philadelphia, Pennsylvana, 1879 – 1957, Frank Furness. Furness was one of the few architects of his generation who went beyond the eclecticism of the day to forge a highly personal system of design and ornament. This relatively small building was executed when his command of integrated form, structure and ornament had matured fully. The site is now a parking lot.

164. AMERICAN LIFE INSURANCE BUILDING   (also known as The Manhattan Building) Philadelphia, Pennsylvania, 1888 – 1961, Will H. Decker. Another of the exuberant and picturesque nineteenth - century buildings, like the Provident Life and Trust, torn down in the process of recreating an eighteenth-century frame for Independence Hall and its companion buildings.

**165. Detail, AMERICAN LIFE INSURANCE BUILDING. The high quality of late nineteenth - century craftsmanship and the respect shown for materials were well - illustrated in the corner pier of this building.

166. Marshall Field Wholesale Store Chicago, Illinois, 1885 / 7 – 1930, Henry Hobson Richardson. Richardson brought to Chicago the gospel of strength, structural integrity, and freedom from dependence on motifs borrowed from the past. If within a few years Chicago architects had gone far beyond him in the exploitation of new materials and new techniques, they referred over and over again to the Marshall Field building as a touchstone for their own designs. Demolished.

167. ADAMS POWER STATION Niagara Falls, New York, 1895 – 1965, McKim, Mead and White. For this major industrial commission, the firm eschewed the fashionable Roman and French forms followed in homes for their wealthy clients and returned to the powerful rhythms and harsh stoniness learned in Richardson's office. This was the first power plant designed to produce alternating current. Its generators were made by Westinghouse, and an international commission of experts served as consultants on the design of its machinery. When it was judged obsolete by the Niagara - Mohawk Power Company, serious attempts were made to preserve it as an Electrochemical Museum and Hall of Fame. Demolished.

Architectural historians debate whether the first skyscraper was erected in Chicago or New York. But to most of the world, Chicago is the cradle of the modern office building. The conditions for its development may have been decreed by the moneymen who demanded fireproof construction, maximum use of real estate and floor space, and plenty of light and air for all offices, but it was the architects who created out of the economic prerequisites the clean, hard aesthetic that formed the basis of modern architecture. Forty years ago the complete history of the structural and artistic development of that architecture could still be traced on the streets of Chicago. Now preservationists are struggling to save the surviving monuments of the Chicago School. Adler and Sullivan's Auditorium and Burnham and Root's Rookery seem safe under the protection offered by official "Chicago Landmark" designation; and the last Adler and Sullivan office building left in the city, the Old Chicago Stock Exchange, has at least gained a temporary stay of execution. But they have become jewels in a not altogether compatible modern setting. Too many of the buildings that made up the sprawling, massive, masculine city of the early twentieth century have disappeared, victims of the same economic forces that gave them birth. Even the stockyards are gone.

168. HOME LIFE INSURANCE COMPANY   Chicago, Illinois, 1883 – 1931, William Le Baron Jenney. This was the first building in which the weight was carried completely on the steel skeleton, with the masonry walls acting only as a fireproof and weatherproof curtain.

169. Tacoma Building Chicago, Illinois, 1888/9 – 1929, Holabird and Roche. Its generous fenestration and clear expression of vertical and horizontal structural elements were typical of the best of the Chicago work. It was also the building that introduced the riveted skeleton.

170. Masonic Temple Chicago, Illinois, 1891/2 – 1939, Burnham and Root. The highest building in the world when it was constructed, the Masonic Temple's 20 stories took full advantage of the possibilities for skyscraper construction that had been created by the introduction of the passenger elevator in 1857 and the development of skeleton framing in Chicago only a few years before. The ornamentation of the top stories was perhaps overdone, but in the clean, functional lines of the shaft the architects formulated design ideas that would be adapted and developed by such moderns as Mies van der Rohe.

171. SCHILLER BUILDING   (also known as the Garrick Theater Building) Chicago, Illinois, 1891 / 2 – 1961, Adler and Sullivan. In the same block as the Masonic Temple, at the same time, rose the Schiller, perhaps the finest expression of Louis Sullivan's vision of the skyscraper as a "proud and soaring thing." The Schiller featured both Sullivan's rich and individualistic ornament, and, in its theater, the magnificently engineered acoustics for which Adler had gained renown. The cornice was removed some ten years before the final demolition of the building. In the foreground is the Borden Block, done by the firm in 1879 / 80, just before Adler took Sullivan into partnership. It, too, has been demolished.

172. DETAIL, cornice   Old Chicago Stock Exchange, Chicago, Illinois, 1894 —, Adler and Sullivan. Only a few years before the Schiller Building was lost, a concerted effort saved Adler and Sullivan's Auditorium. In 1971 the fate of the Stock Exchange, the third of the firm's great Chicago office buildings, was still uncertain as preservationists marshalled both aesthetic and legal arguments on its behalf.

173. TRUST COMPANY OF GEORGIA Atlanta, Georgia, 1891–1971, John Wellborn Root. For the leading commercial city of his native state, Root designed the South's first skyscraper. It was not, perhaps, one of his best buildings, but its bold piers and strongly etched entranceways stood out with authority among the nondescript buildings around it. It is being replaced by a new office building and plaza.

174. THE ARCADE Cleveland, Ohio, 1890 – remodeled in 1939, John Eisenmann and George H. Smith. The Arcade is really three buildings in one, two nine-story office buildings connected by a skylighted five-story arcade of shops and offices. Although it still stands, its two fronts, especially that on Euclid Avenue, have, in effect, been lost by a somewhat thoughtless "modernistic" remodeling.

175. STERLING AND WELCH STORE Cleveland, Ohio, 1908–1968, J. Milton Dyer. Arcades and light courts were popular features of large nineteenth-century commercial buildings. The admission of overhead light to the center portion of the structure made possible more intensive use of the inner space in an era when artificial light could not be depended on. Demolished.

176, 177. LARKIN BUILDING   Buffalo, New York, 1904–1950, Frank Lloyd Wright. Here Wright used the light court, not as lobby or passage, but as the integral core of an administration building. The work centered on the floor of the court and the balconies around it. Elevators, stairs and service facilities were relegated to the corner towers. The building was a sort of fortress, shutting out the industrial environment around it and concentrating on interior spaciousness and order. Its genius was recognized by critics in Europe, but few in America appreciated it while it stood. It was razed, almost inadvertently, to create a parking lot.

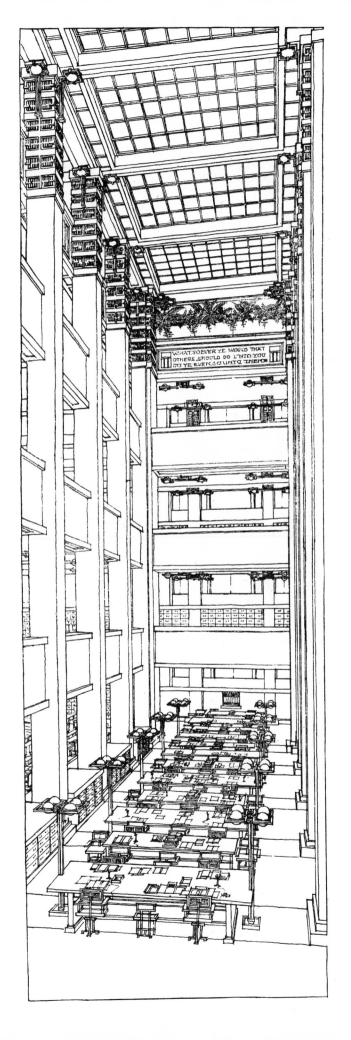

WHATSOEVER YE WOULD THAT
OTHERS SHOULD DO INTO YOU
DO YE EVEN SO UNTO THEM

165

V. Travel & Accommodation

No country has accepted new, faster and more convenient modes of transportation with greater enthusiasm than the United States. The steamboat, the railroad, the automobile, the airplane — each was developed and utilized here with singleminded thoroughness. Perhaps this is simply because we have so much distance to cover. Perhaps it is because we always have been a remarkably mobile people. Having all come here as immigrants, we have no tradition of being tied, either temporarily or permanently, to one place.

The repeated process of replacing outmoded forms of trans-portation with newer and faster systems has had the concomitant result of the continuing destruction and replacement of those structures and institutions that serve the traveler. The wayside inn gave way to the palace hotel, an American invention. First of the breed was Isaiah Rogers' Tremont House in Boston, with rows of rooms opening off long corridors and elegant and luxurious public rooms. The "American" bars and "American" barbershops of the great European hotels are a lingering tribute to the origins of the genre.

The same demand for comfort and convenience that inspired our great hotels has been responsible for their destruction as they age. The process seems likely to continue. We may admire the picturesque, rambling old wooden resorts, but few of us choose to stay in what we regard as firetraps. We expect private baths with every room, reliable heating, air conditioning in hot weather. It is almost impossible today to obtain maintenance and service personnel to keep up the generous spaces built in an era when labor was cheap. One executive of a major hotel chain has stated that the current life expectancy of even a modern hotel is 20 years. So we can expect that more of the old ones will go, except for those few, like the Greenbrier or New York's Plaza, that have acquired the aura of legend.

178. PENNSYLVANIA STATION   New York City, 1906 / 10 – 1963 / 6, McKim, Mead and White.

At each successive American frontier, roads were poor and travelers were few. Accommodation for them was frequent, because each day's journey was short. But the inns were small, domestic in scale and their comforts were sometimes rudimentary.

180. PENNSYLVANIA HOUSE   Irvine, Pennsylvania, c. 1840 – early 1930's. Used by raftsmen floating lumber down the Alleghany, this was given a touch of distinction by the verandahed portico rising a full three stories.

179. INNS ALONG NASSAU STREET   Princeton, New Jersey, from c. 1750 – 1939. Princeton was an important stop on the New York - Philadelphia stage route. Its main street once had some half dozen inns which served as overnight stopping places for stage passengers. The building to the left of center was the Nassau Inn, c. 1760; the larger dormered Federal structure was the Mansion House, 1836; that at the far right was the Washington Arms, c. 1750. All survived until destroyed for a Neo-Colonial complex of shops, offices, apartments, and a new hotel.

In the first half of the nineteenth century both private individuals and the government turned their energies to knitting the new country together with a good system of roads. Rivers were spanned, many of them with wooden truss bridges. Often the bridges were roofed, not for the romantic tunnel effect we admire today, but for the very practical purpose of protecting the span from the weather. Many of these covered bridges, in all sections of the East, have been destroyed by age or flood, or replaced by modern spans.

181. Covered Bridge   vicinity of Hopkinton, New Hampshire, 1863 – 1936.

182. Covered Bridge   Contocook, New Hampshire, 1853 – 1935.

183. Covered Bridge   Cynthiana, Kentucky, mid - 19th c. — mid - 20th c.

184. Covered Bridge   National Road, Indianapolis, Indiana, 1834 — 1902, William H. Wernweg.

From the time Boston's Tremont House opened in 1829, American cities vied with one another to build the most luxurious of hotels. In the pre-automobile age these were located downtown, conveniently close to the stage depot or railroad station. They functioned not only as accommodation for travelers, but often as the most fashionable setting for businessmen's luncheons, meetings of civic groups, and evening entertainments.

185, 186. CHARLESTON HOTEL
Charleston, South Carolina, 1839 – 1960, Reichardt. The Greek Revival hotels of the South were among the most beautiful and luxurious in the country. Richmond and New Orleans also boasted handsome examples of the genre. With its verandah bounded by fourteen Corinthian columns, the Charleston building was one of the last survivors of its type. Demolished, as the picture indicates.

187. GENERAL WORTH HOTEL   Hudson, New York, 1836 – 1970. Even small towns followed the example of the Tremont House. Hudson, a whaling port and center of river trade, was no exception. With the destruction of the General Worth, only two examples of the Rogers - type hotel remain, his old Astor House, in New York City, now much altered by conversion to commercial use, and the Bangor House in Bangor, Maine.

188. BURNET HOUSE   Cincinnati, Ohio, 1850 – 1926, Isaiah Rogers. The fame of the Tremont House brought Rogers hotel commissions from all over the country. For the Burnet House, he moved his office and residence to Cincinnati. Its reputation was worldwide. In 1859 *The Illustrated London News* expressed the wistful hope that a hotel of like quality might be built in that city. Demolished.

189. MAXWELL HOUSE   Nashville, Tennessee, 1859–1961, Isaiah Rogers. By the time he designed the last of his hotels, Rogers had abandoned Greek forms for more fashionable Italianate motifs. The result is perhaps not as felicitous as his earlier hotels. Nevertheless, the building was well-planned in a functional sense. The cuisine, too, must have been good. At least the hotel has gained a sort of immortality on the strength of its coffee. Burned.

190. CAPITAL HOTEL Johnstown, Pennsylvania, 1860 – c. 1960. Originally built to house workers at the Cambria Iron Company, this was the only hotel in Johnstown to withstand the flood of 1889. It was razed for a parking lot.

191. Norse Room   Hotel Pitt, Pittsburgh, Pennsylvania, 1909 / 11 – 1968. John Dee Wareham of the Rookwood Pottery Company of Cincinnati, Ohio, one of the foremost American art potteries of the late nineteenth century, created this dazzling tour - de - force using his company's wares.   It was razed, along with the rest of the hotel, to create a site for a parking lot.

192. CLAYPOOL HOTEL Indianapolis, Indiana, 1902–1969, Frank M. Andrews. This was built on the foundations of an earlier prominent Indianapolis Hotel, the Bates House of 1852, where Lincoln spent a night on the way to his inaugural, pausing to address the town's citizens from the balcony. Although the Neo-Renaissance design of the Claypool was somewhat top-heavy, the entrance facade was dignified and its appointments ranked it among the nation's best hotels. The site is now a parking lot.

In the second half of the nineteenth century the United States grew explosively, in area and population. The railroads grew at a like pace, tying together new settlements and old with ribbons of steel. By the turn of the century, the railroads were expressing their power and wealth in passenger terminals that rivaled commercial buildings and seats of government as the most impressive structure in countless cities and towns. The causes of the decline of the railroads after the Second World War are diverse and complex. One result of that decline is clearly visible — the abandonment or destruction of small town depot and big city terminal alike.

194. BROAD STREET STATION   Philadelphia, Pennsylvania, 1882 / 1892 / 4 – 1952 / 3. Wilson Brother and Company, Furness, Evans and Company. The addition, in this case, became the tail that wagged the dog, the older section being the smaller one shown at the right. The passenger terminal was encompassed only by the space defined by the large windows of the second and third floor. Appropriately, the rest of the structure was designed as an office building, since it performed the function of housing the main offices of the Pennsylvania Railroad. Not one of Frank Furness' more inspired or original designs, it was considerably enlivened by the lavish use of terra cotta sculpture by Karl Bitter. It was taken down to clear a site for the Penn Center development.

193. RELAY RAILROAD STATION   Baltimore, Maryland, 1872 – 1950. The name was a relic from the days when the cars were drawn along the track by horses. This was the first stopping place outside of the city where a pause would be made to hitch up a fresh team. The charming stone Gothic building with its polychrome roof was originally built by the Baltimore and Ohio Railroad as the Viaduct Hotel.

195, 196. CHICAGO AND NORTH WESTERN RAILWAY PASSENGER DEPOT   Milwaukee,
Wisconsin, 1889 – 1968, Charles Sumner Frost. Described when it opened as ". . . the
most convenient, finished and elegant passenger station in the West . . . ," this was
sold by the railroad to Milwaukee County in 1964. Although the Milwaukee
Landmark Commission and other preservationists argued for its survival as an
outstanding example of the Richardsonian Romanesque and the golden age of
railroading, it was razed for freeway construction.

197. "Big Four" Depot Springfield, Ohio, 1911 – 1969 / 70. Like other railroad stations of the late nineteenth and early twentieth century, this fell victim to new modes of transportation in more ways than one. Its site is now occupied by an overpass for Interstate - 72.

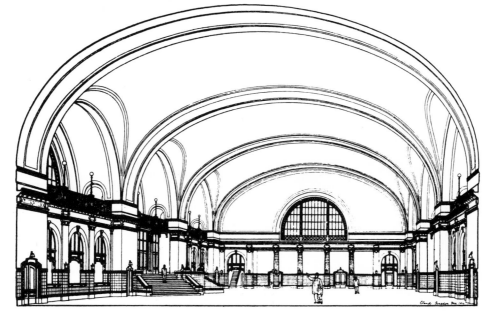

198, 199. New York Central Railroad Station   Rochester, N.Y. 1914 —, Claude Bragdon. In a highly effective expression of the railroad station as train shed, Bragdon designed the great triple arches of the waiting room to echo the forms of the driving - wheels of a steam locomotive. The ornament, in brick, terracotta, faience, and iron, owes a debt to classical models. But it is a free and personal interpretation of traditional forms by Bragdon, an early admirer of Louis Sullivan, and a designer of books and theatrical settings, as well as buildings. The station was partially demolished in 1966.

200, 201, 202. PENNSYLVANIA STATION New York City, 1906 / 10 – 1963 / 6, McKim, Mead and White. The greatest monument of that new empire, the American railroad, was based on the Roman Baths of Caracalla. Despite its monumental colonnaded facade, the most impressive part of the station was the concourse, where seemingly limitless space was confined and shaped, not by the masonry of imperial Rome, but by the steel and glass of the machine age. Even when the station was built, its relatively low height was an expansive gesture of conspicuous consumption. At the height of their power, it was a luxury the managers of the Pennsylvania Railroad could afford, the best advertisement of the railroad's affluence and might. Modern management viewed the site differently, as just another piece of real estate. The tracks remained; the station above them was razed and an office building and a new Madison Square Garden erected on the site.

As roads were built and railroad track was laid, Americans began to travel for pleasure. Getting there was still not half the fun. Stagecoachs were bumpy and the early railroads, burning wood or soft coal, showered their passengers not only with filth, but with live sparks. So early resorts were near the centers of population, and since the journey to them was arduous, stays in one spot were long. The hotels at the seaside, the spas, in the mountains, were large and luxurious and offered ample facilities for promenades, for balls, and the gentle recreations of the nineteenth century. Vacation patterns have changed. The automobile and the airplane offer the opportunity for variety, for short trips to exotic spots. One by one, the great nineteenth - century resorts are giving way to the ski lodge and the motel.

203. THE COURT INN   Camden, South Carolina, 1830 – 1965. Built as a private home, this became an inn in 1889, providing accommodation to tourists seeking good hunting and pleasant bridle paths. Damaged by fire, it closed in 1963. Although plans for its preservation and restoration were discussed, it has been demolished.

204. BRANDYWINE SPRINGS HOTEL   Brandywine Springs, Delaware, c. 1830 – 1916, Thomas U. Walter. Taking the waters
was considered beneficial for young and old in the nineteenth century, or at least a medicinal excuse for indulging in the gay
social life of the spas. This is Brandywine Springs after it had been purchased by the Philadelphia merchant, Matthew
Newkirk, and improved by his architect, Thomas U. Walter. Newkirk's own Greek Revival mansion, with its flanking
dependencies, is shown to the left of the hotel. Destroyed by a series of fires.

GRAND UNION HOTEL
SARATOGA SPRINGS

205. GRAND UNION HOTEL   Saratoga Springs, New York, 1802–1953. In the gilded age of the late nineteenth century,
Saratoga Springs was a name to be reckoned with as one of the great playgrounds of the rich. They came, nominally, to take
the waters, but spent their money at the racetrack. Foremost among its hotels, both in age and elegance, was the Grand Union,
a mammoth extension of the small hostelry built by Gideon Putnam in 1802. In the 1870's it was given a fashionable,
Frenchified Second Empire exterior by E. Doubleday Harris. By the early twentieth century fashion had passed Saratoga by.
No longer economically viable, the Grand Union was torn down.

206. CRESSON MOUNTAIN HOUSE   Cresson, Pennsylvania, 1880–1916. Medicinal springs, pure water, and clean mountain air were the attractions for a health resort founded at this Alleghany mountain site in 1854. They were attractions powerful enough to entice such summer visitors as Charles Sumner and President Benjamin Harrison. In 1880 a new hotel, described in a contemporary brochure as " . . . a very striking structure of the Queen Anne style of architecture blended with Oriental . . . ," was built on the site. It had a few successful seasons, but operated at a loss for fourteen years before it was abandoned in 1897. In 1916, following a fire, the remains of the building were razed. Some of the building materials were used in construction of summer cottages and a cowbarn.

207. ADIRONDACK LODGE   Clear Lake (now called Heart Lake), vicinity of Lake Placid, New York, 1878/9 – 1903. Roughing it in the Adirondacks must have seemed more authentic if it was done in a log cabin. At least that seems the most logical explanation of the popularity of log construction for private camps and public accommodations. The Adirondack Lodge was the most ambitious example of the genre. It burned in a forest fire. The property, with a subsequent building on it, now belongs to the Adirondack Mountain Club.

THE NEW MAGNOLIA
MAGNOLIA MASS.

208. THE NEW MAGNOLIA Magnolia, Massachusetts, c. 1885 — early 20th century. This was one of a series of rambling, wooden, luxurious hotels that stretched from Swampscott to Rockport along Boston's North Shore. The New Magnolia burned early in the century; the others — The Moorland and The Thorwald in Bass Rocks, Gloucester; the Oceanside at Magnolia; The Ocean House in Swampscott; The Turks Head Inn in Rockport — have gone in the last 15 years, all destroyed by fires, some of suspicious origin.

209, 210, 211. Lake Geneva Inn   Lake Geneva,
Wisconsin, 1911 / 12 – 1970, Frank Lloyd Wright. For a
resort town frequented by wealthy residents of Chicago
and Milwaukee, Wright designed a hotel rather like an
enlarged version of the prairie houses he had created for
a similar clientele. Although it could scarcely be counted
as one of his most distinguished works, the Inn was
evidence of Wright's mastery in the handling of abstract
form, especially in some of the interior details. It had
suffered various indignities before its final destruction.

By the closing decades of the nineteenth century, new methods of transportation were beginning to make major changes in American patterns of living. Intraurban transit systems expanded and sometimes fragmented the cities' commercial areas. These and the development of interurban and suburban railway systems made it possible to live far from one's place of employment. And by the end of the century the automobile had appeared on the streets of America, presaging even greater change.

212. SIXTH AVENUE AND FOURTEENTH STREET STATION   Manhattan Elevated Railways, 1878–1939/43, Jasper F. Cropsey. The building of New York City's rapid transit system in the 1870's opened vast areas of Brooklyn and the Bronx to commercial and residential development. It was no longer necessary for the average man to live within walking distance of work. Fast and cheap transportation freed him to enjoy some of the suburban pleasures once reserved for the comparatively wealthy. Manhattan's elevated railways have all been removed, replaced by subways and buses.

213. BOSTON AND ALBANY RAILROAD STATION   Wellesley, Massachusetts, 1884–1964, Henry Hobson Richardson. A neat and simple waiting room, with a pleasant geometry of curved and angular shapes, was a feature of one of a series of suburban Boston stations built in the days when a railroad would commission the nation's ranking architect to provide for the comfort of its daily passengers.

215. GIRARD AVENUE BRIDGE   Philadelphia, Pennsylvania, 1872/4 – 1970/71, Henry A. and James P. Sims.   A straightforward stone and iron construction, given grace by the decorative cast iron handrail and the graceful lamps.   Considered inadequate for modern traffic requirements and truck weights, it was replaced by a new span.

214. TRACTION TERMINAL STATION   Indianapolis, Indiana, 1904 – 1968, Daniel H. Burnham.   At the time of its construction, this was acclaimed as one of the wonders of the world because of its clear-span lightweight steel truss construction. The seeds of its doom are visible in the lower right-hand corner.   Demolished.

216. Emrichsville Bridge   Indianapolis, Indiana, 1905–1948,
Harry Klausman.

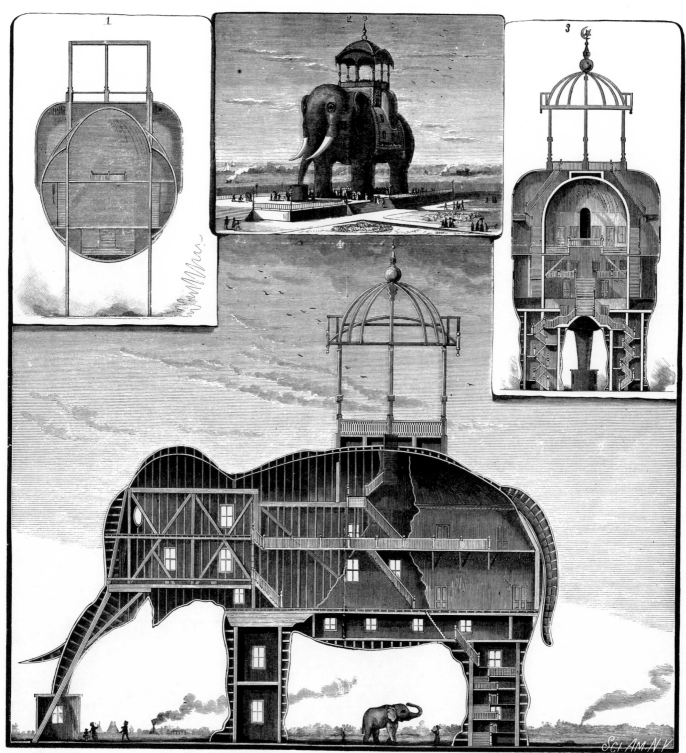

THE COLOSSAL ELEPHANT OF CONEY ISLAND.

VI. Fun & Fantasy

Once a society has gone beyond the pioneering stage and finds some time for leisure, it begins to erect special structures where free time can be spent in the pursuit of entertainment, enlightenment or good fellowship. The designer of such buildings may choose one of two paths. He may follow the prevailing architectural fashions of the day in a manner that does nothing to reveal the special pleasurable uses of the building, or he may find an opportunity to express in his structure the basic idea of fun as an escape into a world different from and gayer than that of everyday.

The former approach might be exemplified by Boston's Old Howard Theater, a building which gained its greatest fame as a burlesque house. It was cast so rigidly in the mold of a Gothic basilica that it is often thought to have been designed as a church, perhaps a unique confusion of the haunt of the ecclesiologist and that of the ecdysiast.

Illustrations of the latter approach are the amusement parks of the late nineteenth century. Here the skeletonized structural patterns were transmuted, in the pavilions and structure of the rides themselves, into lacy and insubstantial toys. Or plaster was used to create fantastic landscapes or buildings molded in the form of grotesques, mythical and real animals, or of human heads. Closely related are the great illusionistic movie houses with their artificial landscapes covered by a canopy of clouds floating past twinkling stars.

Nothing has proved more ephemeral than buildings of this sort. Taste in entertainment has changed very rapidly. Television and the specialized art movie have, to a large extent, preempted the place of the legitimate theater, the movie palace and the lecture hall. More active recreation has replaced the sedate pleasures of an earlier day for both participants and spectators. The crowds flock to the golf course and the football stadium, not the amusement park. The new fantasy is astroturf.

217. ELEPHANT, CONEY ISLAND   Brooklyn, New York, c. 1885 – c. 1900, J. Mason Kirby. When the Coney Island Elephant opened for business, *Scientific American* compared it somewhat facetiously to two contemporary monuments, the Washington Monument and the Statue of Liberty, as one of the eighth wonders of the world. The designer held a patent on the idea. Another of his elephants, at Margate, New Jersey, actually was used as a hotel. It survives, awaiting restoration as a children's library.

Most early public meeting places were small, differing very little in scale or decor from the houses of the neighborhood. With increasing affluence and ease, Americans began to demand elegance and even extravagance as the setting for social events. But meeting places are especially vulnerable to the winds of fashion; what is "in" one year, may well be "out" the next. So some of the most elaborately conceived public meeting places have proved the most ephemeral.

218. MRS. TROLLOPE'S BAZAAR Cincinnati, Ohio, 1829–1881, Seneca Palmer. That critical Englishwoman, Frances Trollope, intended to bring culture to the heathen and make herself a fortune in the process when she conceived her multi-purpose building to house a store, bar, coffee house, private meeting rooms, ballroom and picture gallery. Contemporary visitors, attuned to the monuments of a classical age, found the building "absurd," "grotesque" and "preposterous." To modern eyes, it has a certain raffish charm. The business was never a success. Mrs. Trollope returned to England; her building was put to a series of uses, none of them up to her high cultural standards, before being demolished.

219. TIVOLI HIGH HOUSE Pensacola, Florida, 1805–1930's, Juan Baptiste Casenave, Pedro Bardenave, Rene Chamdiveneau. Built during the last period of Spanish rule, the Tivoli, with its raised gallery, loked much like Spanish Colonial domestic buildings. However, it was a rendezvous for male society, housing the city's only billiard table. Its function may have been more obvious when the round dance hall-theater next door was still standing. That was razed in the 1840's.

220. MAJOR'S HALL Bloomington, Illinois, c. 1854–1959. Almost every small town in mid-nineteenth-century America had its "Hall." Here the townspeople gathered to hear edifying lectures, a concert, or a political rally. Bloomington's was simply a large room on the top floor of a simple, vernacular business block. But if it lacked architectural distinction, it was historically significant. It was the site where Lincoln delivered his "lost speech" in the course of the Lincoln-Douglas debates. Damaged by fire in 1872, it was finally razed for a parking lot.

221. MADISON SQUARE GARDEN New York City, 1890–1925, McKim, Mead and White. Built of yellow brick and white terra cotta and crowned by Augustus Saint-Gaudens' nude statue of Diana, Madison Square Garden was a veritable palace of pleasure. It contained an arena, theater, concert hall, restaurant and roof garden, all testifying to Stanford White's consummate skill as a decorator. Never financially successful, it was demolished and the site developed commercially. At the right is the Leonard Jerome mansion, recently demolished despite designation as a New York City Landmark.

222. MIDWAY GARDENS Chicago, Illinois, 1914, Frank
Lloyd Wright. Commissioned to provide a grandiose beer
garden as an urban center for dining, dancing and staged
entertainment, Wright created an incredible temple to
pleasure, part pre-Columbian, part Cubist. It was
torn down in 1929, a victim of prohibition.

In the urban centers, Americans began to attend theatrical performances in the eighteenth century. By the end of the nineteenth century almost every town of any size had a theater. Sooner or later the traveling companies would fill the house with the latest hit from New York or London, and the brightest stars. As neighborhoods changed, some of these legitimate houses became vaudeville or burlesque theaters. And with the advent of movies, the road show died, and the house lights dimmed for the last time in others. Some survived to show the movies, which also spawned great theaters of their own. In turn, many of the latter have gone, victims of the new amusement, television.

223. HOWARD ATHENAEUM "The Old Howard," Boston, Massachusetts, 1846 – 1963, Isaiah Rogers. Built as a legitimate theater, which opened with a performance of Sheridan's "The Rivals," The Old Howard is probably best remembered as a burlesque house beloved of generations of Harvard undergraduates. The stage was darkened for the last time in 1953. In the early 1960's, when it became known that the building was scheduled for destruction for Boston's new Government Center, friends of the theater and of burlesque, among them Ann Corio, rallied to save it. A fire accomplished part of the work of destruction in 1961 and, although its supporters still thought restoration possible, it was eventually demolished.

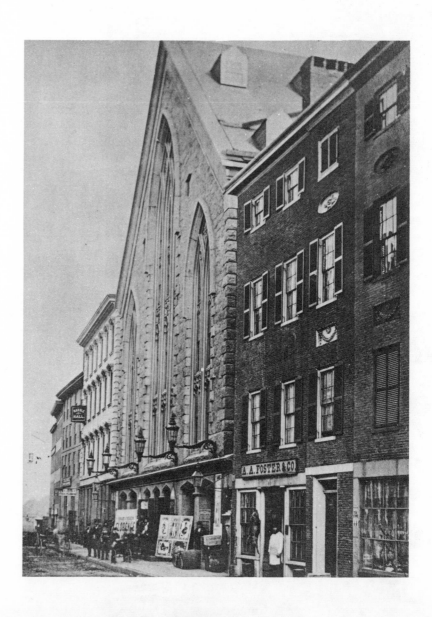

224. ARCH STREET THEATER   Philadelphia, Pennsylvania, 1828–1936, William Strickland. The last of Philadelphia's remaining early nineteenth - century theaters to survive the joint blows of the demise of vaudeville and the Great Depression. Demolished.

225. OPERA HOUSE Pensacola, Florida, 1883 – 1917. In the days when great stars went on the road, people from the entire region filled the Opera House's 1400 seats to see and hear Sarah Bernhardt, Joe Jefferson, Victor Herbert and Anna Pavlova. Severely damaged by a hurricane, it was torn down.

226. GEBHART'S OPERA HOUSE (later Mayfair Theater) Dayton, Ohio, 1876 – 1969, William F. Gebhart. The proprietor of the W. F. Gebhart & Co. Galvanized Iron Works introduced cast iron as a building material to Dayton some ten to fifteen years after it had reached its height of popularity in New York City. His Opera House with its elaborate sheet metal facade over a brick backing was his own best advertisement. It was demolished in the course of a four - block urban renewal project. The zinc statue of the Goddess of Liberty crowning the mansarded tower was rescued and placed on the lawn of the Dayton Art Institute.

227. GRAND THEATER Evansville, Indiana, 1889 – 1962. Now a parking lot.

The great exhibitions of the second
half of the nineteenth century —
New York's in 1853, the Philadelphia
Centennial in 1876, Chicago's in 1893
— seem to have whetted the
American appetite for varied
entertainment in a parklike setting.
Amusement parks in wooded areas or
seaside resorts attracted both the
upper classes and the workingman
seeking an evening's recreation.
Somehow this innocent sort of fun
has lost its appeal. The parks, lightly
constructed of wood and plaster
following the architectural fads of
another day, burn in the off - season.
Or the offers of the land speculators
prove too tempting to owners
watching declining profits. Many of
the great ones are gone or
diminished. Time is running out for
most of the others.

228. RIVERVIEW PARK Chicago, Illinois, 1905 / 6 – 1968. The most extensive amusement park in the Midwest had samples of almost every variety of building common to this fanciful genre – the mill at the right loosely based on a romanticized European prototype; the elaborate, but engagingly flimsy, polygonal carousel; the great slide with its simple geometry of exposed wooden trusses; the structure in the form of a grotesque head beneath the slide. All were razed to make way for a housing development.

229. PIER Long Branch, New Jersey, 1879. When Long Branch was a mecca for both social and political luminaries and day trippers from the city, it welcomed visitors at this lighthearted pier, decked with flags and lights. A number of seaside resorts built such piers to accommodate those who arrived by boat. Many were developed with amusement halls and restaurants. Most have fallen victim to winds and tides.

230. SCENIC TUNNEL, WHITE CITY   Chicago, Illinois, 1904 / 6 – 1939.   Where but in Chicago would an early twentieth - century building for an amusement park be built of cast concrete panels? This one, silhouetted against the prairie sky, had a clean and simple geometry reminiscent of midwestern grain elevators. Less prosaically, it housed what was described as the "great scenic railroad art gallery." The park in which it stood, named for the Columbian Exposition of 1893, also was well equipped with roller coasters and ferris wheels. White City never recovered from an extensive fire in 1927. The remnants went into receivership in 1933; in 1939 the buildings still standing were condemned as a safety hazard and razed.

231. LUNA PARK   Coney Island, New York, 1903–1930's.   Coney Island was the greatest of all American amusement areas. For raucous fun, there was Steeplechase Park, which opened in 1897 and finally closed down in 1964, sold for a housing project.   Dreamland was baroque, full of curved and bulging plaster fantasies. But Luna Park was the stuff of fairytales, a fabulous and almost sedate pleasure garden more akin to European parks like Copenhagen's Tivoli Gardens.   Luna Park – and Dreamland – were destroyed by fires.

VII. Urban Amenities

Most books about architecture deal with single buildings, one by one. This is convenient. It is a method of classifying buildings, of relating them to their own times and to similar structures, in short, of making them comprehensible. But it is not the way in which buildings are experienced visually. In actuality, buildings are seen in terms of their surroundings. And it is the totality — building, site, environment — to which we respond.

By accident or design, the arrangement of buildings in cities can be satisfying to the civilized soul. The city needs to be more than an accretion of hives to accommodate work and living-space. There need to be open spaces, touches of green that place the buildings in proper perspective. There need to be contrast and variety. There need, also, to be unified street facades to define the streets as purposeful thoroughfares, and structures of human scale to remind man that the city is his and not man the city's. Lewis Mumford once remarked that skyscrapers were designed to be enjoyed only by angels or aviators. As our cities, and now our suburbs, get bigger and higher, we need to retain some of our smaller, older structures as reference points both to our past and our own human nature.

There are also the grace notes, too often obliterated or ignored in planning new construction — the odd sculpture, free-standing or incorporated into the fabric of a building at a time when cost per square foot was not necessarily the governing criterion; the fountain, the well-designed lamppost, the mall with benches in the middle of a broad avenue. Above all, we need to preserve a sense of wonder in the city, the opportunity to come around the corner and discover something old, or small, or different tucked away amidst the monuments of a later age.

232. ROWHOUSES Cathedral Street, Baltimore, Maryland, early 19th c. – 1930's. Baltimore was known for its rows of marble-stooped, dark brick townhouses. This row was a pleasant complement to Latrobe's Cathedral. It was razed to provide a building site for the Enoch Pratt Free Library.

City squares were features of those American cities — Philadelphia and Savannah, for instance — laid out according to the most advanced planning of seventeenth and early eighteenth-century Europe. Their chief attraction continues to be valid. They offer green areas of respite from the traffic and bustle of the city. And yet, even when they offer an illusion of rural greenery, city squares are basically urban spaces, defined and given coherence by the buildings around them.

233. TOWN HALL AND MARKET c. 1790–1926/7 and FIRST PRESBYTERIAN CHURCH OF THE NORTHERN LIBERTIES (also known as New Church of Campingtown or Dr. Patterson's Church) c. 1805–c. 1850, Philadelphia, Pennsylvania. When these buildings were erected the Northern Liberties was a separate community not yet integrated into metropolitan Philadelphia. Here the square was not part of a formal plan as the Philadelphia squares were. It was a fortuitous result of the widening of the street to accommodate the market. The placing of the headhouse, stalls, and church created, however, an urban space of some authority. By mid-century the congregation seems to have abandoned their sanctuary for a newer edifice; shifts in street alignments destroyed the impact of the square; the market itself survived until the present century, a relic of an era when city dwellers could purchase produce fresh from the farm devoid of cellophane prepackaging.

234. WASHINGTON SQUARE Philadelphia, Pennsylvania. The original plan drawn for William Penn's city on the Delaware called for the provision of five green open squares. Despite attempts to protect them as early as the 1830's, three of the five have been bisected by streets. Washington Square remains, but the destruction of such buildings as John Haviland's First Presbyterian Church (1820–1939), has done much to diminish the spatial qualities of the square. The building heights are now too uneven, and the sheltered feeling of an enclosed, protected space has been disturbed.

235. St. John's Park   New York City, 1803 – 1867. New York was less mindful of the human condition than Philadelphia. In 1801, the city was laid out in a relentless grid. Only a few sites escaped; one was the small park in front of John McComb's St. John's Chapel. In 1867 the city sold the park to Commodore Vanderbilt, who used its acreage for railroad siding and a freight terminal. The remaining residents fled. The church and a few neighboring houses remained standing until 1918 when they were destroyed during a street - widening project.

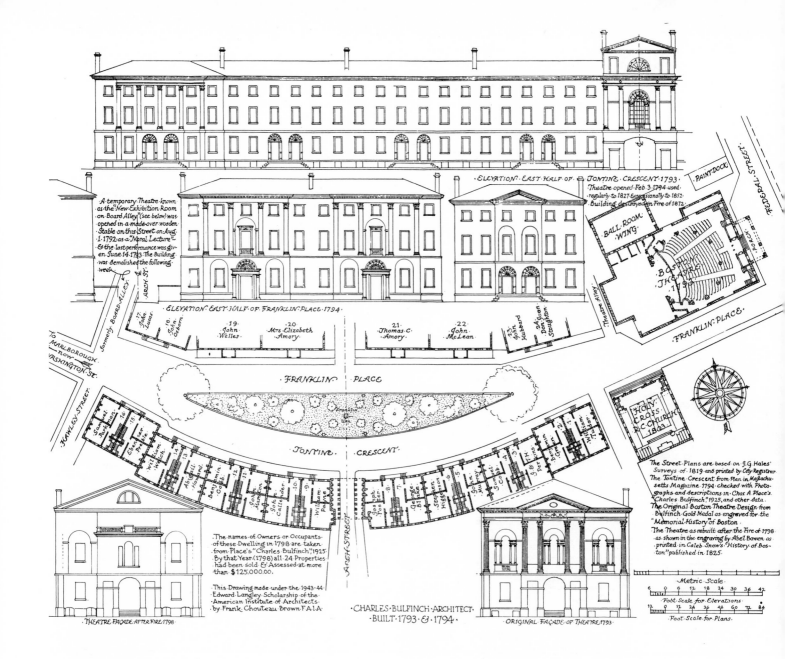

ELEVATION · EAST · HALF · OF · TONTINE · CRESCENT · 1793

Theatre opened Feb. 3, 1794 used regularly to 1827 & occasionally to 1852. Building destroyed in Fire of 1872.

PAINT DOCK

FEDERAL STREET

BALL ROOM WING

BOSTON THEATRE 1793

A temporary Theatre known as the "New Exhibition Room" on Board Alley (see below) was opened in a made-over wooden Stable on this Street on Aug. 1, 1792 as a "Moral Lecture" & the last performance was given June 14, 1793. The Building was demolished the following week.

ELEVATION · EAST · HALF · OF · FRANKLIN · PLACE · 1794

Theatre Alley   PORCH   FRANKLIN · PLACE.

17. John Lucas   18. John Osborn   19. John Welles   20. Mrs. Elizabeth Amory   21. Thomas C. Amory   22. John McLean   23. John Hubbard   24. Jonn Don Juan Stoughton

To MARLBOROUGH now WASHINGTON ST.

HAWLEY STREET

· FRANKLIN · PLACE ·

Franklin Urn

HOLY CROSS R.C. CHURCH 1803

· TONTINE · CRESCENT ·

The Street Plans are based on J.G. Hales' Surveys of 1819 and printed by City Registrar.
The Tontine Crescent from Plan in Massachusetts Magazine 1794 checked with Photographs and descriptions in Chas. A. Place's "Charles Bulfinch", 1925, and other data.
The Original Boston Theatre Design from Bulfinch Gold Medal as engraved for the "Memorial History of Boston".
The Theatre as rebuilt after the Fire of 1798 as shown in the engraving by Abel Bowen as printed in Caleb Snow's "History of Boston" published in 1825.

The names of Owners or Occupants of these Dwelling in 1798 are taken from Place's "Charles Bulfinch," 1925. By that Year (1798) all 24 Properties had been sold & Assessed at more than $125,000.00.

This Drawing made under the 1943-44 Edward Langley Scholarship of the American Institute of Architects by Frank Chouteau Brown, F.A.I.A.

· THEATRE · FAÇADE · AFTER · FIRE · 1798 ·

· CHARLES · BULFINCH · ARCHITECT · · BUILT · 1793 · & · 1794 ·

· ORIGINAL · FAÇADE · OF · THEATRE · 1793 ·

· Metric · Scale ·
· Foot · Scale · for · Elevations ·
· Foot · Scale · for · Plans ·

236, 237. TONTINE CRESCENT Boston, Massachusetts, 1793/1803 – 1858/1872, Charles Bulfinch. In its day, this was the most sophisticated urban design in America, comprising theater, ballroom, church, what we would call today condominium apartments, and later the Boston Library. Most of it was destroyed for business buildings in 1858; the remainder burned in the great Boston fire of 1872.

238. CHESTER SQUARE Boston, Massachusetts, c. 1850.
This pleasant nineteenth-century square still exists, and
is, in fact, enjoying a modest revitalization, thanks to
its attractions for those members of the middle-class
who still enjoy city living. Nevertheless, its peaceful,
residential character has been shattered by the extension
of Massachusetts Avenue through its center.

239. FAYETTE PARK Syracuse, New York. Once this was one of Syracuse's choice residential areas, lined with Greek
Revival and Victorian houses whose occupants could enjoy the sedate pleasures of the central garden. As residential patterns
in the city changed, the houses were first converted one by one to commercial use, and then razed, again one by one, for
business buildings. The process began about the time of World War I. It will end shortly when the last of the houses, now
being used as headquarters for an urban renewal project on the periphery of the park, comes down as planned.

240, 241. COPLEY SQUARE Boston, Massachusetts. Few small American cities offer such architectural riches as Copley Square where Richardson's Trinity Church and McKim, Mead and White's Boston Public Library face one another across the plaza. Those two remain, and the replacement of the old Boston Museum of Fine Arts by the Copley Plaza Hotel did little to break the unity of the square. More damaging has been the demolition of the row of Victorian houses on the fourth side of the square and the substitution of much taller, flatfaced, nondescript modern buildings. The loss of S. Edwin Tobey's S. S. Pierce Building for construction of the Massachusetts Turnpike has opened one corner of the square, destroying the finite, and readily comprehensible enclosure of the space by the buildings around it.

Among the more attractive survivors occasionally to be found in cities are the small urban houses, reminders of an era when most of the business of life was conducted on foot, and the city was a place for ordinary folk to live as well as to work.

242. WEST HULL STREET HOUSES   Savannah,
Georgia, late 18th / early 19th century — late 1930's.

243. MILK STREET HOUSE   Newburyport,
Massachusetts. Modest early eighteenth-century houses like these are sought after today.
In 1940 when the three were for sale for $400,
nobody wanted them and they were demolished.

Once when the streets of eastern cities were lined with solid row of three and four-story buildings it was possible for the traveler to tell at a glance where he was. Each city — New York, Boston, Philadelphia, Baltimore — had its distinctive variations on the basic house type. Now that the skylines are dominated by the steel and glass boxes of the new International Style, that sense of identity has been lost, except in microcosm, in some areas, of some cities.

244. SEVEN BUILDINGS Washington, D.C., 1794/6–1958. This was one of Washington's first rows of substantial houses, an attempt to give the streets of the Federal City the same kind of uniform, dignified facade that could then be found in Philadelphia, Boston and New York. The buildings attracted tenants in keeping with their dignity. When the Federal Government moved to Washington, the State Department was located in the corner building; later it housed the Madisons while they waited for the burned White House to be restored. The group began to deteriorate around 1900. It was, in effect, destroyed piece by piece by radical changes to rooflines and trim. There was little left that could have been saved when the buildings were finally razed.

245. 510 - 524 KING STREET   Alexandria, Virginia. This was a row of Federal buildings which had suffered alterations over the years, although the fine doorways of 518 - 20 and 522 - 24 were relatively intact. The Historic Alexandria Foundation urged renovation and restoration of the group, but were told it was not "feasible" because of parking requirements. The group was demolished in 1970 as part of an urban renewal project. The site is still vacant.

246. 312 - 14 KING STREET   Alexandria, Virginia. Two early buildings which had been through a "modernization" in the mid - nineteenth century. They were demolished in 1968.

Alexandria, Virginia, is a city which has worked hard, often with good cooperation from city officials, to save its historic buildings. Nevertheless, big chunks of the civic fabric have been lost.

247, 248. CINCINNATI, Ohio, c. 1840. These selections come from a panoramic view consisting of eight daguerreotype plates, a pioneering effort to capture an entire city with a camera. What the camera saw were neat rows of commercial buildings along the river with the spires and towers of the town's important buildings rising above them. Still higher, the hills beyond the city formed an acropolis for the temple - houses of the town's wealthy citizenry.

Not all the contrivances that add to the pleasures of life are urban, of course. There are structures and plans that enhance the pleasures of the countryside with all of man's art and skill.

249. COCKLOFT SUMMERHOUSE   Newark, New Jersey, c. 1750–1859. In the days before air conditioning permitted men to seek relief from the heat indoors rather than out, summerhouses and gazebos were far more common. The one at Cockloft Hall belonged to Gouverneur Kemble in the early nineteenth century, at which time it was a favorite haunt of Washington Irving and others of the New York literati. Irving spoke with fondness of its appurtenances. It was furnished with easy chairs; there was a fishpond outside the door so that the gentlemen might be spared the 100 yards' walk to the Passaic River; best of all, it had its own wine-cellar.

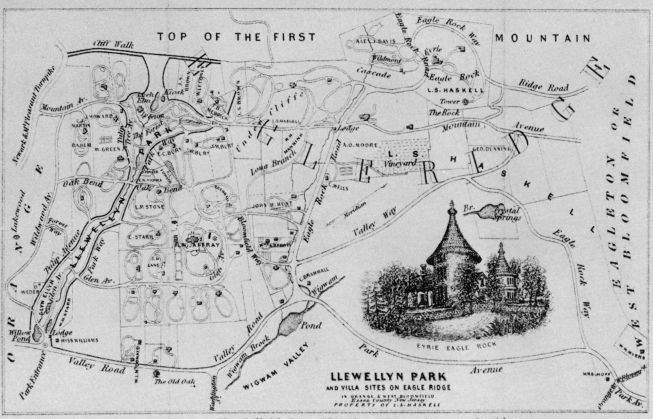

LLEWELLYN PARK

TOP OF THE FIRST MOUNTAIN

LLEWELLYN PARK
AND VILLA SITES ON EAGLE RIDGE
IN ORANGE & WEST BLOOMFIELD
Essex County New Jersey
PROPERTY OF L.S. HASKELL

EYRIE EAGLE ROCK

500 Acres of land, divided into Villa Sites, of 5 to 10 Acres, each, with a
Park of 50 Acres, reserved, for the exclusive use of the owners of the Sites.

250. LLEWELLYN PARK   West Orange, New Jersey, 1853 –, Alexander Jackson Davis. One of the first planned suburbs in America where natural beauty was both carefully cultivated and allowed to remain undisturbed, Llewellyn Park was the most ambitious creation of one of the leading apostles of the picturesque. Fortunately, it is not entirely lost. The winding roads are still there, the trees, the Ramble. But the plot sizes are somewhat smaller and the several castles and cottages that Davis designed for his nineteenth-century suburbanites are, with two exceptions, gone.

*The civilized and sophisticated
city provides for all human needs.*

251. RAY OWEN'S STAR MANSION   Storyville,
detail, gable.

252. STORYVILLE   New Orleans, Louisiana, 1860–1940. Storyville started as a middle-class residential district. By the turn of the century it was one of the most famous red-light districts in the world, covering the 36 square blocks from Basin Street to Robertson, between Iberville and St. Louis Streets. It was out of this setting, from the down-at-the-heel Victorian mansions, and the tawdry streets, that jazz first came. Storyville has been replaced by a public housing project.

253. PUBLIC COMFORT STATION   Indianapolis, Indiana, 1910–1963. Foltz and Parker.

If the metropolises of the eastern seaboard were characterized by their neat ranks of rowhouses, the typical residential streets of the Midwest were broad, tree-lined boulevards, on which each house stood in its own spacious grounds.

254. EUCLID AVENUE   Cleveland, Ohio. This was one of the great boulevards, and from 1845 to 1900 it was built up with a succession of ample and gracious homes. By the turn of the century the long, slow decline had begun. Business began to expand from downtown along the avenue. The wealthy in turn moved further from the center of the city. And as taxes and maintenance costs soared, the big houses and spacious lawns were too expensive to keep up. By 1960 the Euclid Avenue of private homes was gone.

255. AMASA STONE HOUSE   Euclid Avenue, Cleveland, Ohio, 1858.

256. HURLBURT HOUSE   Euclid Avenue, Cleveland, Ohio, 1855.

257. EAST BROAD STREET Columbus, Ohio. Another midwestern "grand avenue," with mansions in the various styles, from Greek Revival to Neo-Colonial, fashionable from about 1840 to the early 1900's. Like Euclid Avenue's, these great houses have gradually given way to commercial buildings.

258. ENGLISH OPERA HOUSE AND HOTEL Monument Circle, Indianapolis, Indiana, 1880 and 1884 – 1950, J. M. McElfatrick &
Son; additions and alterations, 1896, Oscar D. Bohlen. The majority of American cities, especially in the central flatlands, are
laid out in the monotonous regularity, so useful to the real estate speculator, of the grid plan. One of the chief attractions of
Indianapolis is the convergence of its main street on a great circle, around which, although not necessarily on, are clustered
the State House and the city's other major public buildings. Once the sweep of the circle was enhanced and its scale made
both more monumental and comprehensible by this crescent of four - story buildings with their punctuating gables and
towers. The site is now occupied by a tall office building.

259. LAKE SHORE DRIVE Chicago, Illinois, c. 1880 – c. 1955. The great glory of Chicago is its lake front which offers visual relief from the almost endless prairie to the west, cooling breezes in the summer, and the delights of an endlessly shifting landscape of water, cloud and sky. The icy blasts in the winter are another matter. By the early 1880's the industrial barons of the fastest growing city in the country saw the attraction of the shore. They vied to commission the country's leading architects to design manorial homes befitting their wealth and the site. There was Richard Morris Hunt's chateau for William Borden in 1884, H. H. Richardson's fortress for Franklin MacVeagh in 1887, and the pacesetter of them all, Henry Ives Cobb's Potter Palmer House of 1882. In the 1920's these were joined by luxury apartment houses, and Chicago's Gold Coast, along with New York's Fifth and Park Avenues and San Francisco's Nob Hill, became a synonym for wealth, fashion and luxury. In 1949–51, when Mies van der Rohe's pristine glass towers went up at the lower end of the Drive, they seemed to announce the opening of a new post-war era of elegance. The promise has not been fulfilled. As the last of the private houses of the drive have gone, they have been replaced by third-rate, formula apartments in pink and pale blue glazed bricks. In place of the Gold Coast, Chicago now has instant Miami Beach.

260. Potter Palmer House   Chicago, Illinois, 1882 – 1950, Henry Ives Cobb.

Acknowledgments and Credits

"This book could never have been written without the assistance of . . ." is a truism that in this case happens to be entirely true. It is the product of the cooperation and help of scores of professionals and amateurs interested in the preservation of the man - made environment. To detail the contribution of each would be impossible. Nevertheless, special thanks are due to Lawrence Grow, editorial director of the Pyne Press, who suggested this book's theme and title, and whose faith and support have been invaluable at every stage of its compilation. Charles E. Peterson, of Philadelphia, generously shared the wisdom and experience accumulated during some forty years of preservation activity, along with valuable knowledge of places, people and buildings. The National Trust for Historic Preservation has given both moral support and information since the inception of the project. Its staff, in particular Mrs. Terry Brust Morton, Director of Publications and Editor, has been most helpful in making available the record of preservation battles, some won, some lost, during its 25 years of existence. The greatest single source on buildings of the American past is the Historic American Buildings Survey, a division of the National Park Service. Its records, in the form of photographs, measured drawings and written reports, are open to all. In using them, however, I received generous assistance as well as valuable suggestions from numerous staff members, in particular James C. Massey, Miss Nancy Beinke, Miss Caroline R. Heath, Denys Peter Myers and John C. Poppeliers. Mrs. Penelope Harshorne Batcheler and Lee H. Nelson of Independence National Historical Park in Philadelphia, were kind enough to let me examine unpublished material on Independence Hall and the Benjamin Franklin House. Among individuals and institutions who are gratefully remembered for providing suggestions, photographs and information, and for answering sometimes seemingly endless questions with patience are:

Mrs. Alfred W. Dater, Jr., Stamford (Conn.) Historical Society; Melancthon W. Jacobus, Connecticut Historical Society; F. C. Biebesheimer of Norwich, Conn.; Mrs. Gladys M. Coghlan, Historical Society of Delaware; Miss Virginia Daiker, Library of Congress; Robert M. Vogel, The Smithsonian Institution; Mrs. Linda V. Ellsworth, Historic Pensacola (Fla.) Preservation Board; Miss Ruth Kent, St. Augustine (Fla.) Historical Society; J. Reid Williamson and Miss Beth Lattimore, Historic Savannah Foundation; William R. Mitchell, Jr., Georgia Historical Commission; Miss Isabel F. Jarvis of Evanston, Ill.; Vern C. Gray, McLean County (Ill.) Historical Society; James R. Getz, Lake County (Ill.) Historical Society; Miss Ida Blum of Nauvoo, Ill.; Miss Juliet A. Peddle of Terre Haute, Ind.; H. Roll McLaughlin of Indianapolis, Ind.; Robert Braun, Historic Landmarks Foundation of Indiana;

Mrs. Connie G. Griffith, Special Collections Division, Tulane University Library; Miss Peggy Richards, Louisiana State Museum; James B. Vickery, Bangor (Me.) Historical Society; Earle G. Shettleworth of Portland, Me.; Mrs. Anne Parish, Keeper of the Maryland Register; Mrs. Charles Johnson Hansrote, Sr., Allegany County Committee, Maryland Historic Trust; Robert E. T. Pogue, Bushwood, Md.; Wilbur H. Hunter and Paul Amelia, The Peale Museum; George Wren, III, and Miss Elizabeth Beech, Society for the Preservation of New England Antiquities; Mrs. Ropes Cabot and F. Gregg Benjamin, The Bostonian Society; Dr. William D. Hoyt of Rockport, Mass.; J. P. Spang, III, Heritage Foundation, Deerfield; John Herron, Worcester (Mass.) Historical Society; Elliot H. Harrington, Waltham (Mass.) Historical Society; Richard M. Candee, Old Sturbridge Village; Miss Dora Cirlot of Moss Point, Miss.; Miss Dawn Maddox, Mississippi Department of Archives and History; Mr. and Mrs. Charles L. Kaufmann, Strawbery Banke, Inc.;

Henry F. Ludder, Jr., Society for the Preservation of Long Island Antiquities; Harley F. McKee of Syracuse, N.Y.; Mrs. Virginia M. Barons, Genesee County (N.Y.) Historian; Mrs. Virginia B. Kelly, Oneida County (N.Y.) Historian; Mrs. Patrick Harrington, The Landmark Society of Western New York; Mrs. David Siedenburg, Cortland County (N.Y.) Historical Society; Richard Wright, Onondaga Historical Association; Mrs. Adelaide R. Smith, Historical Society of the Tarrytowns; Dr. Adolf Placzek, Avery Library, Columbia University; Goddard Light, Rye (N.Y.) Historical Society; John G. Waite, New York Historic Trust; Daniel M. C. Hopping of New York City; Catherine W. Cockshutt, North Carolina Department of Archives and History; Miss Mary Katherine Petlewski, Greensboro (N.C.) Historical Museum;

Daniel R. Porter, Ohio Historical Society; George H. Berkhofer, Clark County (O.) Historical Society; John Large, Jr., Western Reserve Historical Society; Mrs. Francis Forman, Cincinnati Historical Society; Gary D. Schuman, Montgomery County (O.) Historical Society; Mrs. Theodore Sprague, Hudson (O.) Library and Historical Society; Dr. Margaret B. Tinkcom, Philadelphia Historical Commission; Peter Parker, Historical Society of Pennsylvania; Arthur P. Ziegler, Jr., and James Van Trump, Pittsburgh History and Landmarks Foundation; Mrs. Antoinette F. Downing, Providence Preservation Society; Mrs. Helen G. McCormack, Gibbes Art Gallery; Charles Lee and Mrs. James W. Fant, South Carolina Department of Archives and History;

James W. Moody, Jr., and Calder Loth, Virginia Historic Landmarks Foundation; Mrs. Hugh B. Cox, Historic Alexandria Foundation; Mrs. Eleanor Lee Templeman of Arlington, Va.; Mrs. Charles J. Riegers, Jr., Fairfax County (Va.) History Commission; Captain A. A. Fuchsman, Arlington County (Va.) Police Department; Mrs. Nan Netherton, Fairfax County (Va.) Division of Planning; Richard W. E. Perrin and Mrs. Mary Ellen Wietczykowski of Milwaukee, Wis.; and the many others who made suggestions for which there was, unfortunately, insufficient room.

Credits and sources are given in the order in which illustrations appear in the text. Abbreviations have been used in some cases: CAA - G, Carolina Art Association, Gibbes Art Gallery; CHS, The Connecticut Historical Society; HABS and HABS / LC, Historic American Buildings Survey, the designation HABS / LC indicating that these illustrations have been transferred to the Library of Congress for storage; HLFI, Historic Landmarks Foundation of Indiana; HSP, The Historical Society of Pennsylvania; LSWNY, Landmark Society of Western New York, Inc.; MCHS, Montgomery County (Ohio) Historical Society; NJHS, The New Jersey Historical Society; OHS, Ohio Historical Society; PHLF, Pittsburgh History and Landmarks Foundation; SB - P, Strawbery Banke, Patch Collection; SPNEA, Society for the Preservation of New England Antiquities; TPM - B, The Peale Museum, Baltimore; VHLC, Virginia Historic Landmarks Commission; WRHS, The Western Reserve Historical Society.

Cover Louis C. Williams, photographer Frontispiece HABS / LC

Pg. 14 New England Textile Mill Survey: Smithsonian Institution/National Park Service Pg. 16 courtesy of The National Trust for Historic Preservation, Matthew Lewis, photographer.

Introduction: Indian village, Princeton University Library; Revere engraving, LC; painting of State St., courtesy of Massachusetts Historical Society; State St., c. 1850, SPNEA; State St., 1880, Bostonian Society; Old Indian House, SPNEA; Hancock House, SPNEA; Jonathan Hasbrouck House, *Harper's New Monthly Magazine;* Pumping Station, Philadelphia Waterworks, HSP; Albany, N.Y., *Harper's New Monthly Magazine;* Delmas House, courtesy of Miss Dora Cirlot; Residence of Thomas Powell, *Harper's New Monthly Magazine;* Bodleian Plate, courtesy of Colonial Williamsburg, Inc.; Manigault-Gibbes House, CAA-G; Wetter House, Georgia Historical Society, Foltz Collection; Trinity Church, Episcopal, courtesy of Miss Dora Cirlot; Forks of Cypress, HABS/LC; Ossian Hall, HABS/LC; Burned House, HSP; Resurrection Manor, Delaware State Archives; Baldwin-Buss House, courtesy of Hudson (Ohio) Library and Historical Society; Iron Front Buildings, VHLC; Williams-Macon House, LC/Johnston Collection; Maplewood, courtesy of Fairfax County Division of Planning; Port Royal, HABS/LC; St. James St., HABS, Cervin Robinson; India Wharf, SPNEA; Kensington, Russell Maxey, photographer; Heck-Andrews House, State Department of Archives and History, Raleigh, N.C.

I. *Civic Pride* 1. HABS / LC 2. courtesy of Norris F. Schneider 3. Herman Miller Collection, courtesy of Mrs. Charles J. Hansrote, Sr. 4. SB-P 5. HABS-LC 6. courtesy of Mary Ellen Wietczykowski; D. C. Sigerfoos, photographer 7. HABS, Jack Boucher 8. HSP 9. NJHS 10.,11. HABS, Jack Boucher 12. HLFI 13. HABS, Jack Boucher 14.,15. HABS, Allen Stross 16. SPNEA 17. Carnegie Library, Pittsburgh 18. Georgia Historical Society, Foltz Collection 19. HLFI 20.,21. HABS, Allen Stross 22. courtesy of Miss Isabel F. Jarvis 23. courtesy of Eleanor Lee Templeman. 24. Historic Pensacola Preservation 25. courtesy of Miss Isabel F. Jarvis 26. Clark County (Ohio) Historical Society

II. *Faith, Hope & Charity* 27. SPNEA 28. Berks County (Penn.) Historical Society 29. HABS / LC 30. Louis C. Williams, photographer 31. SPNEA 32. CAA-G 33. TPM-B 34. Illinois State Historical Society 35. Wayne Andrews, photographer 36. HABS / LC 37.,38. Worcester (Mass.) Historical Society 39. Louisiana Collection, Tulane University Library 40. Hudson (Ohio) Library and Historical Society 41. Princeton University Archives 42. VHLC 43. HABS, Cervin Robinson 44. HABS / LC 45. Architectural Archives, Oneida (N.Y.) Historical Society 46. State of North Carolina, Department of Archives and History 47. Milwaukee County Historical Center 48.,49. Museum of the City of New York

III. *House & Home* 50. Museum of the City of New York 51. SPNEA 52. Historical Society of Delaware, Annie Reeves Rodney, artist 53. SPNEA 54. courtesy of Goddard Light, Rye (N.Y.) Historical Society 55.,56. Society for the Preservation of Long Island Antiquities 57. State of Delaware, Division of Historical and Cultural Affairs 58. VHLC 59. Jackson County (Miss.) Genealogical Society 60. NJHS 61. HSP 62.,63. SPNEA 64. VHLC 65.,66. SB-P 67. SPNEA 68.,69. SB-P 70. courtesy of Lehigh County (Penn.) Historical Society, a *Call-*

Chronicle staff photograph 71. SB-P 72.,73. Old Sturbridge Village, John O. Curtis 74. Historical Society of Delaware 75. VHLC 76. NJHS 77.,78. HABS / LC 79. State of Delaware, Division of Historical and Cultural Affairs 80. HABS / LC 81. State of South Carolina, Historic Resources Division, Department of Archives and History 82. OHS 83.,84. HABS / LC 85. SPNEA 86. Cortland County (N.Y.) Historical Society. 87. TPM-B 88. HABS / LC 89. SPNEA 90. LSWNY 91. Society of the Founders of Norwich, Conn., Inc. 92.,93. Genesee County (N.Y.), Genesee County Historian 94. HABS / LC 95. OHS 96. HABS / LC 97. courtesy of Juliet A. Peddle 98.,99. HABS / LC 100. Enoch Pratt Free Library, Baltimore 101. NJHS 102. Avery Library, Columbia University 103. HABS / LC 104. SPNEA 105. courtesy of Norris F. Schneider 106. Bangor (Me.) Historical Society 107. Onondaga Historical Association 108. Greensboro (N.C.) Historical Museum 109.,110. NJHS 111. TPM-B 112. The National Trust for Historic Preservation

113. CHS 114. SPNEA 115. PHLF 116. VHLC 117. CHS 118. LSWNY, Paul and Sally Gordon 119. OHS 120. MCHS 121. Randolph Langenbach, photographer 122. NJHS 123.,124. HABS / LC 125.,126. Architectural Archives, Oneida (N.Y.) Historical Society 127. Wayne Andrews, photographer 128. MCHS, Rollyn Putterbaugh 129. VHLC 130. WRHS 131.,132.,133. HABS / LC 134.,135. Museum of the City of New York

IV. *Commerce & Industry* 136. Buffalo and Erie County (N.Y.) Historical Society 137. Stamford (Conn.) Historical Society 138. HABS / LC 139. Warren County (Penn.) Historical Society 140. HABS / Allen Stross 141. St. Augustine (Fla.) Historical Society 142. Fairfax County History Commission 143. HABS / LC 144.,145. courtesy of Dr. Thomas H. Gandy 146. HSP 147. CAA - G 148. Historic Savannah Foundation 149. Bangor (Me.) Historical Society 150.,151.,152.,153. SPNEA 154. HABS, Detroit Edison Co. photograph 155. The Adirondack Museum 156. Smithsonian Institution 157. HABS, Cervin Robinson 158. New York State Historic Trust 159. HSP 160.,161.,162. CHS 163. HABS / LC 164.,165. HABS, Ned Woode 166. Chicago Architectural Photo Co. 167. HABS / LC 168.,169.,170.,171. Chicago Architectural Photo Co. 172. HABS / LC 173. Georgia Historical Commission, Bob Irwin 174.,175. WRHS 176.,177. *Ausqeführte Bauten und Entwürfe von Frank Lloyd Wright.* Berlin: Wasmuth, 1910.

V. *Travel & Transportation* 178. HABS / LC 179. courtesy of the Princeton University Library 180. Warren County (Penn.) Historical Society 181.,182., 183. HABS / LC 184. HLFI 185. CAA - G 186. courtesy of the Charleston (S.C.) *News and Courier* 187. HABS, Jack Boucher 188. Cincinnati Historical Society 189. Tennessee State Library and Archives 190. Cambria County (Penn.) Historical Society 191. PHLF 192. HLFI 193. TPM - B 194. City of Philadelphia, Records Department 195.,196. courtesy of Mary Ellen Wietczykowski 197. Clark County (Ohio) Historical Society 198.,199. LSWNY 200.,201.,202. HABS, Cervin Robinson 203. Camden (S.C.) District Heritage Foundation, Ross E. Beard, Jr. and Richard T. Dunlap 204. courtesy of private owner 205. courtesy of George S. Bolster 206. Cambria County (Penn.) Historical Society 207. from the Collection of Maitland De Sormo 208. SPNEA 209. courtesy of Mary Ellen Wietczykowski 210.,211. HABS, Richard Nickel 212. New-York Historical Society 213. HABS / LC 214. HLFI 215. HABS, James Cremer 216. HLFI

VI. *Fun & Fantasy* 217. from the Collection of Frederick Fried 218. Cincinnati Historical Society 219. Historic Pensacola Preservation 220. McLean County (Ill.) Historical Society 221. New-York Historical Society 222. Chicago Architectural Photo Co. 223. SPNEA 224. courtesy of The Franklin Institute, Philadelphia 225. Historic Pensacola Preservation 226. MCHS 227. courtesy of *The Evansville Courier* 228. from the Collection of Frederick Fried 229. NJHS 230.,231. from the Collection of Frederick Fried

VII. *Urban Amenities* 232. TPM - B 233. HSP 234,235. New-York Historical Society 236.,237.,238. SPNEA 239. Onondaga Historical Association 240. SPNEA 241. The Bostonian Society 242. HABS / LC 243. SPNEA 244. National Trust for Historical Preservation 245.,246. Historical Alexandria Foundation 247.,248. Cincinnati and Hamilton County (Ohio) Public Library 249. NJHS 250. Avery Library, Columbia University 251., 252. Louisiana Collection, Tulane University Library 253. HLFI 254.,255.,256. WRHS 257. OHS 258. HLFI 259.,260. Chicago Architectural Photo Co.

Index